Chippenham

Memories

Chippenham

Memories

Ruth Marshall

TEMPUS

Cover picture: Crowds gather in Chippenham Market Place on VE Day, 8 May 1945.

Frontispiece: Unveiling of the Chippenham Borough War Memorial on 4 September 1921. The dedication psalm was read by the Venerable. R.T. Talbot, Archdeacon of Swindon. The memorial was unveiled by Councillor A.M. Stevens, Mayor of Chippenham Borough. A commemorative wreath was then laid by George Wood and Reginald Neate, two ex-servicemen. Field Marshal Lord Methuen gave the final address.

First published 2005

Tempus Publishing Limited
The Mill, Brimscombe Port,
Stroud, Gloucestershire, GL5 2QG
www.tempus-publishing.com

© Ruth Marshall, 2005

The right of Ruth Marshall to be identified as the Author
of this work has been asserted in accordance with the
Copyrights, Designs and Patents Act 1988.

British Library Cataloguing in Publication Data.
A catalogue record for this book is available from the British Library.

ISBN 0 7524 3511 6

Typesetting and origination by Tempus Publishing Limited.
Printed in Great Britain.

Contents

Babs Foster (*née* Alison), Ruth Cousins (*née* Hadwin), Joan Bryant (*née* Jackson) and Shirley Ritchens (*née* Alves) collecting for the Chippenham Carnival.

Acknowledgements

I would like to thank the officers of Chippenham Town Council and the Museum and Heritage Centre Management Committee for readily agreeing to act as a partner in the implementation of this project. On a more personal level I would like to thank Elaine Full, Deirdre Clague, Rob Catt and Howard Harding for assisting with the many interviews that took place to get the Oral History Project started. My thanks also to Frank White, Don Little, Margaret Smith and Peggy Chamberlain for assisting with corrections and to Gillian Minter for proofreading the final manuscript. I would also like to thank the wardens and volunteers of the Chippenham Museum and Heritage Centre, who have been involved in various ways in this project and to everyone who agreed to be interviewed and to lend their personal photographs. My apologies to those whose interviews did not get published. I hope that all who read this will enjoy the lively reminiscences that it contains and that it will jog the memory of many Chippenham residents past and present. The Oral History Project will continue and many more interviews will be recorded, hopefully to be available as audio memories in the galleries of the museum at a future date. It is important that memories are preserved and valued. Many things have changed during the lives of the contributors to this book and I hope that this book will provide a valid record of everyday life in Chippenham over the last century. My thanks to all who have supported the process of the production of this book in any way, however small.

Foreword

The Oral History Project came about from an awareness of a lack of documented accounts of life in Chippenham. The book is the result of many hours of interviews, transcriptions and editing, to which the staff and volunteers of the Chippenham Museum and Heritage Centre have been central.

Working on an oral history book is a bit like starting a jigsaw puzzle without having any idea of what the finished picture will be! You start with isolated stories about a whole range of things, people and places you have never heard of (not coming from Chippenham doesn't help!), but as you progress with the interviews, stories start to connect and you start to hear different versions of similar incidents and places. Fragments connect and you start to get an idea of some of the smaller pictures within the whole. Having never heard of Billy Gee or Gaffer Hinton, I can now confidently connect them with local schools and I know that Bonnie Freegard and Champion were well known around the town of Chippenham as they delivered to one and all!

Chippenham has been a thriving market town for many years and the memories of its inhabitants document an era that saw much change and development. The years of the Second World War had a substantial impact on both the area and its people. The post-war development of the retail areas of the High Street and the Market Place brought the loss of some beautiful buildings and very few local people view the loss of the Town Bridge in a positive light, despite the reduction in flooding that the river development brought.

Working with the staff and volunteers of the Chippenham Museum and Heritage Centre, the oral history project has documented the personal lives, experiences and views of a range of Chippenham people. Some describe an era that will be unrecognisable to younger readers. A time when not only did mobile phones not exist, but when all calls were connected manually by the operator. A time when the results of the Eleven Plus examination dictated your level of education and access to a 'better' job. And a time when you spent five years as an apprentice learning a trade that would last a lifetime.

Many things are different today and it is important and worthwhile to document and record what life was like in the past and how much things have changed. The memories in this book are, as far as possible, as spoken by the interviewees. Limited editing has been done only to ease the flow of what has been said and I hope that readers will 'hear' the local dialect as they read the individual accounts and will enjoy the often amusing anecdotes and glimpses into the past. The full recordings and transcripts will be held by the museum and will hopefully be available to the public in various ways in years to come.

My thanks to Mike Stone and the staff of the Chippenham Museum and Heritage Centre, the wardens and volunteers and all who agreed to be interviewed as well as to those who helped to record the many interviews that have contributed to this book. Thanks to all who have lent precious photographs and items to be included for publication. Thanks also to the museum for permission to use a range of previously unpublished photographs to accompany the text.

Ruth Marshall
January 2005

Introduction

The story of the origins of this book starts with the move of the museum collections from the Yelde Hall to the new museum in 2000. In the summer of 2001 the museum staff, working with heritage students from Wiltshire College, Chippenham, mounted an exhibition on the Second World War in the temporary exhibition galleries. As the exhibition was researched it became clear that there was a lack of published accounts of the happenings to the military and the community of Chippenham, particularly in the Second World War. A small oral history project was created with informal interviews, which were edited and displayed in a written form in the exhibition. The results of this project demonstrated a continuing need to record the oral history of an ageing population, but with museum expansions looming the project was put on hold.

In 2004, an oral history book was proposed and we secured the services of Ruth Marshall and quickly recruited a team of volunteers from the Museum and Heritage Centre wardens and commenced the oral history project. The local media was used to advertise for members of the Chippenham community to make themselves known. The initial response was strong and continued through most of the year. Ruth Marshall and her team carried out interviews in people's own homes and at the Museum and Heritage Centre.

At the beginning of the project the museum staff hoped that the oral histories would provide information relating to a wide range of activities and interests within the local community. The collected information would help to build on the significance of the social context of the collections, which we hold in care for the community. The completed recordings and transcripts will be stored at the museum and hopefully be added to and available for public access. The information can also be used in future exhibitions and will be fundamental in helping the museum to understand the significance of local objects, documents and recorded events.

As the project progressed through the year the chapters evolved into seven areas. Many of the oral histories referred to similar events like the Second World War, school days and work at the Westinghouse Brake and Signal Company. Towards the end of the project a get-together was organised at the museum and many of the people who had given oral histories came along and brought photographs and documentation for possible inclusion in the book. Where there were gaps, previously unpublished photographs were selected from the archives of the Museum and Heritage Centre.

The following text and pictures have succeeded in carrying out the project tasks. The two longest sections on the war years and working life are particularly useful in creating a picture of what life was like in Chippenham in the recent past. They contain many humorous accounts and interesting views. These memories are now recorded both in print and on tape and form an important additional resource in the Museum and Heritage Centre, which we hope to add to in the future. I am sure that the reader will enjoy the accounts of what happened to people in the Chippenham community as much as I have. Finally I would like to thank Ruth Marshall and her team and the many members of the Chippenham community who have helped to create worthwhile book and permanent archive of people's memories and histories.

Mike Stone

Manager and Curator, Chippenham Museum and Heritage Centre

one

Childhood

Richard Wiltshire and Terence Goddard stride down the High Street with their mothers.

Seasonal games

Games you played when you were a child used to change like the seasons. Used to have a spell of hopscotch, a spell of the skipping rope, a spell of taking a hoop and a piece of stick to make it roll along. All games like that. It was lovely! I was an only child, so I used to have to make a lot of my own amusement, I always used to do that at school. The games were the same, like we used to have − so-called netball, but you didn't have the nets then. You had to just fling it, and try and get the person to stop it going in towards the goal. I never used to play hockey until I came to Chippenham, and I never enjoyed it! I was looking out for the ball, watching the sticks, because I didn't want to be getting hit! That was the main thing.

Jean Brind

John Coles Park

At that time you could go out into the ro[a] and play hopscotch and ball games and hoo[p] Everyone in those days had a metal hoo[p] with a piece of wire that you hooked roun[d] it, and you ran up and down the road wi[th] it. John Coles Park played a big part in o[ur] lives, because they were all young families [in] those days, down the road. We would spen[d] many hours up in John Coles Park. I was th[e] youngest of the family, and quite often m[y] sister was sent up to fetch me home, when [it] was time to go to bed. But I mean in tho[se] days, you made your own fun.

John Lovelo[ck]

Observing the Sabbath

We visited my grandparents on a Sund[ay] and that was a great treat because grea[t] grandfather would have nothing done [on] a Sunday. Even the china and that, was n[ot] washed up. The only thing that was wip[ed] clean was the cutlery, because it was th[e] steel cutlery and that had to be wiped cle[an] and dry, otherwise it rusted. Other than th[at] nothing, but nothing. Vegetables, everythi[ng] had to be done on Saturday. No newspape[r] on Sunday. The fact that newspapers we[re] printed Saturday night didn't matter − [he] would not have one that was printed Saturd[ay] night to be delivered Sunday, because Sund[ay] was the Sabbath. I can remember them as [a] very kind couple, but very, very strict and [it] was a very strict upbringing. And of cour[se] we were very sedate in those days, we we[nt] in and great-grandfather would come in an[d] say 'Sit by me' and he always had a pouffe [by] him, you know, and you sat and you we[re] seen and not heard. You took a book wi[th] you, or something, because you didn't dare [do] knitting on a Sunday, or sewing, anything li[ke] that. A book was tolerated.

Ivy Wa[rd]

...eeting in John Coles Park are Margaret Clark, Peggy Chamberlain (*née* Beynon), Mavis Whale, Margaret Comley and ...an Hale, May 1941.

...aying inchy-pinchy

...used to play in St Mary Street and around ...e churchyard. My mother would meet me ...om school with a picnic and we'd go down ... Westmead also and play inchy-pinchies ...d skipping rope games and all that, and ball ... against the chapel wall in Emery Lane. ...chy-pinchy – well, you stood at the end, ... the pavement, and they would say do so ...any inchy-pinchies – which were very tiny ...tle steps. Or else you would have to do so ...any paces, which were bigger ones – or else ...ou had to go back so many steps, so that ...e first one that actually got to the end of ...e road won the game. We used to delight ... going along St Mary Street and knocking ... a window where there was a parrot in a ...ge, belonging to Mr Pollard, who was the

town bailiff. He was a big tall man with a long white beard and his wife was a little lady and she used to wear a lace cap and black clothes. Of course we used to make the parrot squeak and squawk. He used to come out and tell us off. Then the man would come along with the rod to pull the gas lamps on, of course the boys would go along just after him and put them back up so the lights weren't on! We were naughty! We used to tie bits of cotton onto people's doorknockers and things. Whips and tops and marbles and in the autumn, we used to collect conkers and put matches in them and make little chairs and furniture and cotton reels of course, the French knitting we used to do. We used to have wonderful times.

Margaret Smith

Don Little pictured with his bicycle at Biddestone.

Cut cheese!

There was another game we used to play. Where the school is up there and right along the edge of the playground, there was steel railings and we used to play a game called 'cut cheese'. You used to draw a line in the gravel, and then you took it in turns to jump, and the one that jumped the farthest was called 'cut cheese', and the one that jumped the least had to bend down and the others would leap-frog over and as far as they could in front of you. Then they'd draw another line and you'd move up to that one and then you had to go from the first line to that one in one step and then do your jump, and then you'd keep on moving up and up and up till you were up to three steps or something like that of 'cut cheese'. And everybody that wasn't jumping used to stand and watch, and if the one that was jumping just missed the line, if his foot went over the line, everybody would shout 'cut cheese'. Innit daft!

Norman Beazer

A birthday in hospital

My fourth birthday was in November an I had this abscess on my neck. It was rour about my birthday because I was in hospit for that, but they wouldn't allow my paren to see me. I was in hospital for a fortnig and I didn't see my parents at all. They cou look in the window at me, but they couldr come in to see me. I was in this cot and was in a ward where there was a lot of grow ups and everything, and I know I cried ar cried and cried and all the toys they gave n I whipped over the side of the cot. Because was the youngest I was spoilt! On the day my birthday, all new toys came in from n parents and everything and I didn't chuck or of those over the side of the cot. I must ha known it was from my parents. That was tl Cottage Hospital, in London Road, which now demolished.

Peggy Chamberla

A choirboy

When I was a boy in Ivy Road, we used to g to the Baptist church. When my mother w having us children, my Aunty Frances looke after us in a little tiny cottage in Ivy Cottage There was a wooden hut in the Woodlan Road, that was a Nissen hut from the Fir World War and that had been made into church. I wanted to go to church, so I thir my sister, my brother and I went to that churc and that's where we got confirmed. Attache to this church was Hardenhuish church. I use to go to Hardenhuish church – there we sixteen boy singers in their church choir wii four or five men and the vicar there, I ca remember his name now! Reverend Carter loved the singing and still do.

Brian Tinso

Postcard view of the Cottage Hospital in London Road.

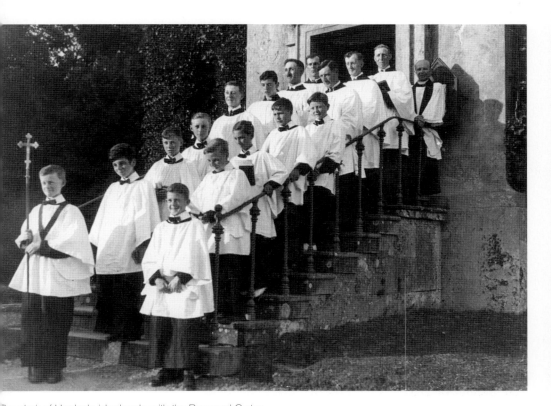

The choir of Hardenhuish church, with the Reverend Carter.

Home-made sweets

On the corner, where the council offices are now, was a sweet shop – Mr Burton. He made all his sweets right up at the top of St Mary's Place, opposite the Black Horse, over a little road, and he had his sweet factory up there and he used to make home-made sweets, home-made lollipops, and we used to get a toffee lollipop. I think they were about a ha'penny each.

Norman Beazer

Rhubarb and custard

There was Mrs Strange, on the corner, and you used to get five toffees for a ha'penny and ten for a penny, and of course sherbet dabs we used to have, and gobstoppers – you had to put them out to see what colour they were! And liquorice things and rhubarb and custard, I remember, and raspberry drops. Humbugs, yes all those sweets, all in jars.

Margaret Smith

Peggy Burgess (*née* Gribble) at eighteen months of age, photographed at Craston's Studio, New Road, Chippenham in 1942.

Church collection

We used to go to Sunday school up at St Paul's. We had a penny or tuppence for collection. There was a shop on the corner there, Frost's I think the name of it was – a greengrocer's. I remember outside there was always a slot machine with toffees, and quite often, I'm afraid, that's where the penny or tuppence would go! I can remember the organist lived down St Paul's Street – Mr Swaine or something. He was quite strict mind, with the schoolboys, course he always had a mirror up in front. In fact most of the organists do, so that they can see when they got to stop playing, and if you were messing around he would see you. You'd get a whack across the hand! We used to go on pretty well without anything much happening. As choirboys we went to weddings – got paid for them, that was the best part about it!

John Lovelock

An impatient lady

Mrs Swaffield's on the Shambles. She wasn't a very patient lady. Because you only had a penny and a ha'penny. I used to get a penny pocket money. She was not very patient and we used to go in there and it was quite a decision to know what sweets you were gonna buy! Good gracious me! And she was 'Come on, hurry up, hurry up, hurry up'. Oh dear – in the end you had to sort of pick and you'd get outside and think 'Well I didn't really want them!'

Peggy Chamberlain

Sunday school party at St Peter's, Lowden, with the Reverend Brain in the 1950s.

The paper round

I started doing a paper round when I was about thirteen, and I done a paper round until I left school. I done a morning paper round for Langley's paper shop in Audley Road, and then in the evening I worked for a Mr Hall, delivering evening papers.

Norman Stacey

A fascination with balconies

We always went to Sunday school. Then as we got older, we joined the Church Guild and some of the girls joined the church choir. I remember – there were four of us and Sunday evening we used to go to all different churches, you know test them all out. We went to the one in the Causeway, the one in St Mary Street and St Andrew's. The ones around the area – the Wood Lane-London Road area. The ones that used to fascinate me was the congregational ones because they had balconies, and we used to go up into the balcony – and get told off for talking!

Peggy Chamberlain

Earning a penny or two

Well there was a big house at the top of Emery Lane, Alexandra House where Mr Singer used to live. He had a housekeeper there and she had a little girl. She was a dwarf, the little girl and we used to go up and stand at the window ledge and talk to her. And then the

Peggy Chamberlain (*née* Beynon) down Westmead,
c. 1934.

and she used to give me a penny for doing nothing to spend in the sweet shop – Mr Curley's sweet shop in Timber Street, or Mr Swaffield's.

Margaret Smith

Saving for Meccano

We had a toy shop. When you get to the top of the High Street where the road divides, that there was a very high class gents' clothing shop and there was a Miss Hulbert, she had the toy shop. And that was a dream of a shop … you know what I mean, and we used to save up because Meccano was the thing. There was all steel strips and pieces that you built up and you made it into anything. You used to save up to buy so and so and she'd sell a little bit at a time see. She had a list of what it cost. Miss Hulbert – funny old lady.

Norman Beazer

Confirmation class

I went to St Andrew's with Sunday school and church guild and we went to confirmation classes with dear old Mr Green – the vicar. We used to have confirmation classes in the kitchen. Well Peggy and I used to giggle and he separated us, she had to go one end and I had to go the other end. He was a dear old chappy. Every week you got a beautiful stamp to put in a blue cover book and I think – twenty, you had to collect. Also I remember the Sunday school Christmas parties. We had a party in the church hall and it was always Punch and Judy – I hated Punch and Judy. And you had a bag of sweets and an orange and a cake, with tea with buttered buns and cake and that sort of thing. I had one little book when I was in the very small Sunday school class, from Mrs Curley's daughter. I've still got it at home.

Margaret Smith

mother come out and said 'Do you want to earn a penny?', so we used to say 'yes', and we used to have to get all the weeds out between the pavement and up against the wall and then we'd get a penny for that! And then there's another lady along – we used to call her Granny York and if we did an errand for her she used to give us a piece of cold figgity pudding and we used to sit on her steps and eat this pudding. And of course I had a granny

two

Schooldays

CHIPPENHAM WESTMEAD COUNCIL MIXED SCHOOL.

Report for the period ending *June 30th 1933.*

Name *Margaret Taylor*   Standard *I.*

Attendances possible *373* Attendances made *373.*

Number in Class *40* Position on Final List *15*

Subject.	Position in Class.	Remarks.
Arithmetic	21	*Tries to improve, but is weak in this subject*
Reading	5	*Good. Nice expression.*
Recitation	14	*Quite satisfactory.*
Composition	16	*Progress made.*
English	17	*Improved.*
Geography	*Good*	*Very attentive in these lessons, and always*
Nature Study	*"*	
History		*Answers well especially Nature Study.*
Needlework	10/13	*Was very poor at sewing but improved of late.*
Drawing	11/13	*Depends on the objects, evidently prefers flowers.*
Hand Writing / Science	30	*Letters are unevenly formed*
Hand Work / Domestic Science	*Fair*	*Raffia better than Paper Work*

Conduct and General Remarks *Generally quiet, and truthful.*

Class Teacher. *S. S. Carpenter.*   [signature] Headmaster.

School report for Margaret Taylor (*née* Smith) in 1933 from Westmead School.

Children at Lowden Church of England School, in the 1920s.

A village school

I went to school in Biddestone for a while, in the old school by the pond. I think there were only two classes – there were the juniors in one room and then the older ones in another.

I think there was just two teachers – a Miss Smith who looked after us younger ones and her mother I think had the post office! – and the headmaster ran the other class. I think his name was Wyles. But he used to walk every day from Corsham to Biddestone, used to stride up to the village.

Then I came into Chippenham to St Paul's – I think Miss Oliver was the headmistress there – and eventually to Ivy Lane. Mr Greenwood I think was the head then. One character down here was Mr Palmer. That was wartime, you might know they converted the railway arch by Ivy Lane School into an air-raid shelter. Blocked up the ends with bricks. Everybody – when here was a warning – disappeared in there! Wasn't very nice. It was bricked up and dark.

David Hall

Singing with the school

I went to Lowden School. Got on very well. A very good school we had. Lowden School was known for its country dancing. I think Ivy Lane was the sports school and Westmead was swimming. Otherwise we also had singing – a Mr Dear was the headmaster. He was the organist at Lowden, St Peter's church. He used to take some of us, those he thought could sing I suppose, and we'd go round and sing carols for the church at Christmas time and we would go round to sing Easter praise. I loved choir. At Whitsuntide, Mr Dear used to take us down to the Lowden church and of course we'd sing hymns and everything like that. Did games and everything at school. Boys played their own games and girls played their own games. The girls really were more for dancing than games I think. Boys of course played football and we had gardening too. You were allowed to do a little bit of gardening and plant certain things – trees and vegetables, which were very nice.

Lowden School group, *c.* 1947. The children's clothing and letters suggest they were working on a project about the Post Office.

You stayed at that school right through your school life. Right until fourteen.

Amy Brand

Absent from school

I went to school at Lowden School. I didn't go there very long because, unfortunately, I had what they called in those days CSM, cerebrospinal meningitis, which they call the meningococcal now. So, I had a year off school. And when I went back to school it was only for a matter of a couple of months, and I had a fireside chair with a board across the arms, because I wasn't allowed to sit on a hard desk because of my spine. And two boys were delegated to take the chair from room to room when we changed classrooms, which didn't make me very popular really. So it was quite hard work.

Ivy Ward

A truant in trouble

St Peter's School wasn't very far from where I lived — Lowden. There's a stream running down the side of the school — Ladyfield Brook I think it's called. I can remember one day was missing one afternoon and the headmistress contacted my mother and they tried to find out where I was. I was down in the brook along with two other boys playing in the brook, like children do! I got into an awful lot of trouble, from the headmistress, my mother ... and also my father when he came home!

So I was at the primary school up until I went to Ivy Lane. The way we used to get there was down through Sheldon Road, past what used to be known as Platt's fish and chip shop, then on a footpath which goes across the side of Downing, Rudman and Bent. It used to be known as a brickyard or cinder path because it wasn't hard and if it was raining you used to get muddy. I used to get into trouble going across the cinder path or brickyard. Ivy Lane, we had a headmaster there, his name was

A Christmas group at Westmead School in 1946.

Mr Robbins – he was Scottish. One day of the year – it must have been Saint Andrew's day – he always turned up in a kilt. At the time I couldn't understand why a man wore a skirt! Of course we were very naïve! From there I went to the Secondary Modern school, on Cocklebury Lane opposite the railway station. And I was there up until I finished school at the age of fifteen.

Derek Brinkworth

Not stopped by the weather

I went to school at Lowden in Chippenham. I can visualise myself sat in a classroom. But I remember the winter of '47 when we had all the snow, 'cause only three of us turned up for school. And I was one of the three! And the snow was a good ten inches deep, but I could just about manage to get down from Ladyfield Road into Sheldon Road, the snow was just below the tops of me wellingtons! And that snow hung around for quite some little while.

Then off I went to Ivy Lane School, which was just a normal school. I wasn't that keen on school, but nonetheless I played football and all the various sporting activities. Mr Short was the headmaster when I first went there and then he retired and a Mr Robbins took over. He lived in Yewstock Crescent. One of my teachers was a Miss Rodgers, and there was a Miss Pope. We started to do gardening at Ivy Lane – we didn't do woodwork until I went to the Secondary Modern school.

Norman Stacey

A strict headmaster

I liked Westmead School. A big old brick building, with Miss Bell the art teacher, Mr Robinson, Miss Ryall and Miss Carpenter. Then I remember Miss Lymington, the headmistress. There was Miss Cole, Miss Carpenter and Miss Ryall. And then I went from the Infants across to the Juniors and Mr Penny – the headmaster. He was a terror, very straight and he was a tall man. Very strict. We had to stand in line for morning assembly and he used to go down the line with his cane, switching his trouser leg with a cane! And he used to cane boys, because I've heard them in his staff room with the swish of the cane. I remember we used to go to school in a morning and there's a little bakehouse, just before the school – Mr Hunt's bakehouse – and if you had a ha'penny you could buy a little tiny cottage loaf, all nice and hot from the bakehouse, and if you were rich and had a penny you could have a nice sticky lardy cake! Which wasn't very often!

Margaret Smith

Passing the Eleven Plus

Westmead School was in Wood Lane, just down the bottom from where we lived. There was the Infants school – which was on the high bank there and when we were seven we moved over to the big school. When you were eleven, you took the Secondary School exam, which I took when I was ten. I passed, so then I went to the Secondary School – which was in Cocklebury. It was called the Secondary School, which when we moved to the new one it was called the Grammar School. We moved there in 1939 to the new school and oh it was super. It was quite a change from the old tin huts that we were in, in Cocklebury. But we used to enjoy it there, I mean we had the lovely playing fields there. I was eventually in the school netball team and I was in the school hockey team and we also had the four house teams. We played against each other. Rowden, Lowden, Monkton and Avon. I was in Rowden. I think we enjoyed being there, but I suppose as the school got bigger and bigger, we had to move and that was when we went to Har'n'ish. So yes, schooldays – I think they were brilliant, really brilliant. I can't ever remember having been bullied – like they talk about now. Everybody were sort of all friendly

and that. I cycled the first time when I went there, when I was ten. I cycled from London Road and my first day at school I got knocked off my bike by a lorry and I must have broken my collar bone, which I didn't know I did, and cycled on to school!

Peggy Chamberlain

St Mary's Convent School

My birthday was in September, so I would have been a winter child going to school and I must have been a bit of a sickly child, because I think I was always catching colds. I think I got wet walking from Rowden Road round to Lowden School and I can vaguely remember a round stove where clothes were put to dry. I do remember having milk bottles with the straws that you poked through the hole of the cardboard. I don't think I was at Lowden School for very long, but my mother decided and took me up to the convent, which was St Mary's Convent at that time. Catholics and protestants together. I was there until I was ten, when I went on to the Grammar School.

The sisters were very strict, especially Sister Callister, who had this cane kept on the blackboard. It was a big class and we were very well taught and we were given lots of poetry and things like that to remember. Which stood me in good stead, because I could remember reams of things like *Hiawatha* and things like that, when I got to the next school. But one of the best memories – they had a big library of those yellow Rupert books. Every Friday, you were allowed to choose a yellow Rupert book to take home to read.

At the convent the boys had to leave school when they got to eleven, probably, but girls could stay on longer. But my mother wanted me to go off to the Grammar School so I took the exam there at the convent and then went on when I was ten or eleven.

Doris Roddham

Going to the Grammar School

My parents were teachers and I suppose they expected things of me. I started school at St Paul's and I went from there to Ivy Lane. Then you took the Eleven Plus. And I don't know how, but I passed the Eleven Plus. I don't know if by jiggery-pokery or whether it was by cerebral activity! Anyway I went to the Grammar School and as my parents promptly discovered, I spent most of my early life at the Grammar School in the C stream! Happily fooling around, I suppose, and then when I got to the third or fourth year – I saw the light and I started to get more into scholastic activity. I took the School Certificate and did quite well. Then I went on to take Highers and I took four subjects in Highers – botany, physics, zoology and chemistry and I managed to succeed in all of them. I surprised a lot of people! Then I applied for university, and I went on from then to university, to Reading. So for a C streamer, in many ways I didn't do too badly!

Michael Gee

Empire Day

My primary would have been St Paul's School up in Park Lane. It was quite a happy time there. Boys and girls in together obviously. I suppose we must have stayed there until we were about seven or eight. Empire Day was always quite a highlight. You know that was made a lot of in those days. You know, the flags came out and all sorts of things happened. There was Westmead and Lowden School, and

Miss Lansley's class at St Paul's School in Park Lane, 1939.

Ivy Lane, so once a year up in John Coles Park there was sports day. Football – each team played one another. I can always remember that because our team won it that year and I had a medal. That was always a full day – sports day up there you know. Teams running one against the other.

John Lovelock

School in the war years

I started to go to school at St Paul's School in Park Lane. That was during the war and I can remember when the air-raid sirens went, having to go out in the shelter which was in the yard. One thing I can always remember about the school was afternoons or after dinner having to go to sleep. There was like boards and that, we had our own pillows and I just could not abide it. I could never get to sleep anyway and I hated it! From St Paul's School I went to Ivy Lane. I quite enjoyed it. There was quite a bit of travelling because the room in Ivy Lane wasn't sufficient for the number of children there and most of my

classes were either at Monkton Hill Methodist Church hall or Station Hill Baptist church hall. We used to have to go to assembly in the mornings and then troop up to either Station Hill or Monkton Hill. A lot of my main class-rooms were in those two places.

Don Little

The threat of the cane

Unfortunately at that time, I'd missed the Eleven Plus. I was too late to take it in Chippenham, so I went to Ivy Lane School. We had quite big gardens at the back of Ivy Lane then. We were all taught gardening. At school I can remember Mr Hinton – Gaffer Hinton we used to call him! He was very strict. I was left handed, but we were made to write right handed. There was no option. You had to use your right hand. But he was quite strict and the cane was used occasionally. I never had the cane but it was used – it was always the threat of the cane, more than the use of it, wasn't it!

John Lovelock

Class 5 at Ivy Lane School in 1939.

Art with Robin Tanner

School – I don't think I liked school very much to be honest. I can remember Gaffer – we used to call him Gaffer – Gaffer Hinton his name was. First thing in the morning we all had to get in this assembly room. And we all got round this piano and he used to play the piano for our morning prayers. He always had a white handkerchief in his pocket and every now and again he'd wipe his nose and put it back in his pocket. He always got me right in front of the piano. I was a boy soprano and I'm not boasting, but I could sing. We had the cane, mind, as well. Yes I had the cane – I can't remember what for, mind! But the best part of my life at Ivy Lane School was when I got into art. The art teacher – Mr Robin Tanner – used to live in Kington Langley. He was a wonderful artist. Wonderful and he taught me all I know. I was twelve at the time and I did some pictures, some biblical pictures while I was in Mr Tanner's art class, didn't realise he'd kept those pictures from when I was twelve. They had an exhibition at the Holborn – at the end of Pultney Street in Bath – some years ago and I heard that I had two or three pictures there. So Barbara and I jumped in the car and away we goes to Bath and see these pictures.

Brian Tinson

A lack of finesse!

In 1946, I guess, I progressed to Ivy Lane School. Now Miss Pope, I remember, used to teach us country dancing. And in particular, she wanted to teach the boys some country dancing, despite the fact we were so-called 'very clumsy'! And I remember morris dancing with big sticks, which we had to tap lightly, but of course we didn't. We tapped heavily! And an introduction to Scottish dancing, where the crossed swords were on the floor and we had to delicately dance between the swords. Being boys we were very clumsy and they were kicked all over the place, but Miss Pope did not see that we were doing it deliberately. She saw this as just lack of finesse and she carried on teaching us country dancing. Later in our time at Ivy Lane School, because of lack of space I guess, I can remember being marched out of the school to Monkton Park where they obviously had an overspill arrangement and also another place we went to in that area. And I can remember in particular the teachers that we had there – there was a Mr Richardson and a Mr Evans.

Tony Knee

Home for dinner

I can't remember having school uniform, because there wasn't a great deal of money in those days. I know quite a lot of the children used to have milk in school – in Ivy Lane. I don't think there was any dinners there as such, certainly no cooked dinners or anything like that. I always used to come home for dinner. I know we had one teacher, a Mr Greenman, who lived at Hullavington, he was very religious, very strict but very fair. He used to take us for sports up John Coles Park. Well my sister was going up to Secondary School, but I stayed at Ivy Lane until I left. I know she used to come home loaded with homework. I used to think I'm glad I'm not doing that! I left at fourteen.

John Lovelock

Winning a free place

Lady Muriel was Head of Governors, something like that, of the old Secondary School. In those days you had to pay to go there, but every year they used to run a 'free place examination' and if you could pass the 'free place examination', you could go to the school free – apart from buying your uniform. And I passed it and I went up to the old Secondary School till I was fifteen and three-quarters. Then I left school and went to the works.

Norman Beazer

Commercial School

I was going to school at what was called the Senior School up in Cocklebury Road, which is now the college. Later on I took an exam and I went to a commercial school at Trowbridge. I was there for a couple of years. We did shorthand, typing, book-keeping. Together with general subjects as well. After that I was looking for a job.

Frank White

The Secondary School

I went to Ivy Lane School. Got on really well there. In fact I had enough marks in the Eleven Plus to be able to go to the Grammar School, but because there weren't enough places I wasn't able to go. I had to go to the Secondary Modern school instead, at eleven that would have been '51. The Secondary Modern school was nice and it was where the college is now on Cocklebury Road. I remember that we had an entrance at one side for the boys, and the girls to go in at the opposite end and we weren't supposed to go in the wrong way! Mr Minter, Eric Minter, was the headmaster and was very strict, very firm. If he saw anybody running in the corridors, you would be in his office and reprimanded. You'd behave yourself, but it was good. Then we sort of outgrew the school a bit and they had extra classrooms put into the grounds. It was really interesting. The boys had woodwork, the girls had cookery and sometimes if there wasn't space in the school, while they were waiting to get temporary classrooms organised, we actually walked around the town to different part of the town to have our classes. I remember

Staff at Chippenham Secondary School, with the headmaster Mr Newall Tuck seated centre, in the late 1920s.

Boys of the Chippenham Secondary School, 1958, pictured with Mr Davis, Mr Chamberlain and Mr Gee.

that the schoolroom at the Baptist church was used and a room up at St Andrew's church for something else. They had some prefabricated buildings which is now part of the Grammar School and we used to walk all the way up the Malmesbury Road to those. So we had quite a fair bit of walking to do between classes. We had gardening and sewing up there. Miss Webb I think her name was – she was very good. If it wasn't right, she made you take it apart. She was a perfectionist. It stood us in good stead, because I can sew today.

Marian Stickland

Nicknames for the teachers

Discipline – my goodness me! I tell you something – at the Secondary School, in Cocklebury, you went into the gym for assembly and you'd have all the hubbub going and as soon as Miss Morgan or Mr Heckstall-Smith stepped over the threshold, you could hear a pin drop. And we weren't allowed to sit down and when masters or mistresses came into the room, you'd stand up and you did what you were told in those days, because we didn't know any different. There was Smokey Mason, Kipper Davies, well we always said Joe Chamberlain … Billy Gee, he was the science master. Mr Holman. Molly Morgan was the headmistress. I used to cycle from Emery lane to Hardenhiuish with a friend from this end of town, so we used to cycle home together or go to school together on bikes. We were sent for by Miss Morgan – the two of us one day. I said to Laura 'I haven't done anything wrong, have you?', and she said 'No, not that I know of!', and do you know why we were sent to her? Because someone had told her that we took our panama hats off cycling

Chippenham Secondary School football First XI in 1936, with Mr Gee and Mr Jones.

home. Well, they used to blow off in the wind! So our mothers had to sew elastic under the things for us to still wear them! And we were frightened to death that we'd done something wrong!

Margaret Smith

Billy Gee's kid!

In fact the kids at school used to embarrass me – 'Oh there's Billy Gee's kid'. His name was Walter, but everyone assumed that his name was William, and so they'd say 'Aah you're Billy Gee's kid ain't you!' I used to loathe my association with it, because he was regarded … well you can speak to people now in Chippenham and say 'Did you ever come across a teacher called Billy Gee?' and it's either 'Oh not him' or 'Oh yes, he was marvellous!'. I used to hate going out with him. John Coles Park was near the house and

invariably we'd go into town and go through John Coles Park – and you weren't supposed to cycle – and I'd see people that I knew very well, sort of fellow delinquents like myself, and they'd be riding their bike and he'd say 'Come on sonny get off that bike!'. They'd get off and walk and then when I'd see this character later they'd say 'Who was that bloke you were with that told me to get off my bike?' and I had to admit that he was my father.

Michael Gee

A difficult interview

Now in 1949 we had a very big thing in school called the Eleven Plus examination. And of course some of us failed and some of us got through, and I can remember the interview as we were told that the interview was with the headmaster of the Grammar School, who was a very stern gentleman named Mr Farrah

volved with borderline cases. In other words
ve had the academic side and then we were
nterviewed for those last few places. We were
sked impromptu questions and so on. We
vere told what to expect and they were not
ifficult questions, but of course as a youngster
gainst a very stern looking gentleman, who
idn't smile very much and my own teacher
vould have been there. I remember him
sking me where I lived and I said 'Oh, Park
Avenue' and he said 'Where is Park Avenue?'
.nd I had to give him directions, say from the
ailway station and of course you say 'I went
own such and such a road' and he says 'But
 don't know where such and such a road is'.
Ie said 'That's not very clear' and he really got
ne worried and I thought afterwards I'd failed.
But in fact I didn't, so I got through the Eleven
lus and in 1949 I went to the Chippenham
srammar School at Hardenhuish. There are
nany teachers that I remember, because it was

a good time for me. We were introduced to lots
of new things. Being fairly sporty I remember
being introduced to rugby, because all the kids
played soccer. And hockey, and cricket, and in
particular athletics. I have fond memories of
Morgan Perkins, my PT instructor, and as I
say sport was important to me then.

Tony Knee

Breaking the contract

I didn't get a free place to the Secondary
School. You got free places or you had to pay,
so my mum and dad paid for me to go to the
Secondary School in Cocklebury and then I
went up to Hardenhuish in 1939. She paid
three guineas a term for me, so that was twelve
pounds a year and I was supposed to stay until
I was sixteen. I liked school too, except for
the last year and I was so humiliated because
I was bottom of the class in maths! And I was

aff from the Secondary School are among a group enjoying a charabanc trip to Gough's caves, Cheddar, in the late
920s.

so upset because I just could not do algebra and geometry and I cried. I didn't want to go back to school, so my mum said 'Well, you'd better get yourself a job then! You've got to tell your father. I'm not telling him you've left school'. They had to pay seven guineas to take me away, because they broke the contract. So I told my dad I was starting work on the Monday at the Co-op and he said 'How much money are you going to get a week?' and I said '14s 3d'. He said 'Right my girl, then you can pay your mother back ten shillings a week until you've paid her back that seven guineas and then when you've paid that back you can have some more'. But for 4s 3d a week, you could do an awful lot in those days. I had to pay her back and when that was paid back I got more pocket money.

Margaret Smith

Canning's College

I can remember I took my exams. Some go through, some didn't, and there was so man evacuees there wasn't enough places. Ther was a school from London was taking up ha of the Grammar School. Janet, my friend, an myself didn't get through to start with. Jane went on to take it again, but my father ser me to a private school – Canning's College i New Road. It had been on the cards that I wa going to go to Wells in Somerset, because m father went to the Blue School in Wells, bu the war came and that stopped it. So I wer to Canning's in New Road.

Shirley Ritcher

Members of the Secondary Modern School Young Farmer's Club visit Lackham for the Young Farmer's Day, c. 1950.

three

Working Life:
Local Trade
and Industry

A contract at Battle Abbey

My father worked for Downing and Rudman, his trade was a bricklayer and mason. He worked away from home quite a lot, because in those days, most of Rudman's work was restoration work. Old buildings, churches and things. I can remember my father working up in Eton College. He'd come home weekends. 1931, Rudman's had a contract down in Battle Abbey – which was a girls' school there. They had a terrific fire. It didn't burn the place right down, but it did a terrific lot of fire damage and father was sent down there in charge of the job. In those days – he was general foreman, they didn't call them site agents and fancy titles then. You were either a foreman or a general foreman. He was sent down there. I went down with my parents and we lived down there for two years in Battle Abbey in the part that wasn't burnt down.

John Lovelock

Of the 'old school'

My father was a carpenter. He was a ver very skilled man. He worked for Downin and Rudman and in those days, Downing an Rudman used to specialise in period restora tion. They used to go to the big houses an one of the big jobs they did was at Battl Abbey, so that's what he did for a long tim down at Battle. But then when he came back he worked in the workshop over Rudman just across the back there. And of course, da was one of the 'old school' and all his tool everything were shiny, and everything he di was good.

Norman Beaze

A blacksmith's business

The blacksmith's at 21 Gladstone Road wa Billets first, then in 1908 Eli and Fred Kid

Campbell and Wells music shop in 1964, with Bell's confectioners next door.

ook the business over from Billets. Fred Kidd was a member of Chippenham Fire Brigade and on a call in 1928 he was killed in a tragic accident on the Town Bridge. His father, Eli Kidd, gave up in 1929. Henry John (Jack) Martin bought the stock and rented the workshop from Fred Kidd's widow. Then in 1940 I went to work for Jack Martin, my uncle, and when he died in 1953 I took on the business. When Mrs Kidd died in 1959, the premises were sold to G. Flower & Son and the workshop was demolished. I moved my business to Hungerdown Lane, had a new workshop built, and was there for ten years. About 1970 a supermarket wanted the premises, so I sold it and transferred the business to the Old Brickyard, Saltersford Lane. I was there for thirty years and retired nearly four years ago.

John Goodway

Making faggots

was fifteen when I left school and I went and got a job at the Wiltshire Bacon Company, in Foundry Lane. There used to be quite a big factory. I started off just mincing the meat which goes into the ingredients. Then after about a year or two they asked me to go onto the machine which actually makes the sausage meat. I went from there to the faggot department — making faggots! And I was amazed what actually went into faggots! There's a lot of talk, stories, that what goes into faggots isn't very nice, but it's not true! I enjoy faggots even today. Anyway I decided that I wanted to move on, so I got a job with Westinghouse and I worked in the rectifier assembly department.

Derek Brinkworth

A delivery boy

had to get work because my mother being left with us five children, I was the eldest and my youngest sister was eighteen months old. So my mother had to be looked after. I went to work before I left school to be honest. I worked for Mr Fred Evans delivering papers. I would leave the station at six o'clock, every morning — five days, six days a week, I would deliver papers all around the villages and used to ride back into Chippenham, so if I had a puncture or it was raining, pouring or things like that, I would get back mid-morning. I worked there for about four years. Next day you used to take the papers round to the Goods Department at Chippenham Station, and you had to send them back to London where they came from. I went round there one day and the foreman said to me, 'Brian', he said, 'do you want a job on the railway?' And I said 'I can't get a job on the railway'. In those days you had to have someone working on the railway to be able to give a name to say who you are. It was Mr Frank Baker, he was the foreman there and Mr Fred Sutton. And they said to me, 'Go in and see Mr Dibden, the manager, to see if he'll take you on because the lad porter is now going as a signalman'. So I went into see Mr Dibden, had a word with him and told him what I was doing. And he said to me, 'Go back and tell Mr Evans to give a week's notice and start here on Monday week on the station'. So that's what I did.

Brian Tinson

Hulbert, Light and Company

I started an apprenticeship as a carpenter and joiner. My father tried to get me into the joiner's shop at Rudman's but there wasn't a vacancy at that time, so I took it off my own bat and went up to Hulbert, Light and Company in the High Street and got an apprenticeship there. At that time they had just taken over Light's. Up Union Road, was the joiner's shop that belonged to Light's. I remember Mr Light — funny little chap. Old-fashioned. I helped make coffins at that time, but I think Mr Light must have been about ready to retire. After he disappeared the coffin-making went, we didn't make any more then. I certainly helped make a few coffins and it was all by hand to start with. The old gas engine that was in there, was worn out and while I was there electric motors were fitted to the planer, the saw and the other machines. But up until then I can remember slogging away cutting down two inch thick pieces of timber to make things by hand. It was quite hard work. The old foreman was an old chap by the name of Mr Webb, who lived up Sheldon Road, he was the old style, but you learnt your trade there. The bosses used to come round – Mr Park, there was no Hulbert's then, it was Mr Park that was the boss – and they would come in and walk around and look to see what you were making, look at your tools. I can remember one day he picked up my wooden plane and you know, it had a few hammer marks in the front end and I got told off for that, having hammer marks in it. They took an interest in you as apprentices. You bought all your own tools. Father bought them for me. It was a general sort of joinery works. I mean there was no places then not like it is now, where you could go round to Travis Perkins and places like that. There was nothing like that. The firms would have a lorry load of timber in and you would stack it up into the sheds. They were all open-sided sheds so that the timber dried in them naturally. We did a variety of work. I mean, all within a ten-twelve mile radius of Chippenham, but everybody cycled you know. You didn't get taken to work. I remember cycling down to Bath. And if you didn't get there by eight o'clock you were told off! Finish at half past five. Twelve o'clock Saturdays. They had a little bit of a joiner's shop at that time as well at the back of – Hulbert and Light's had a shop in the High Street there, which was taken over after by the saddlers. But at the back of that

there was a small joiner's shop and there was plumber's shop and a stores. The big buildin out the back, that was the store room for th company.

I had five shillings a week for the first yea it went up to 7s 6d the second year. And think it was about twelve shillings and abou a pound for the last year. Once it was the en of the last year, you thought you were rich get ting a pound a week then. Course at the sta of my last year the war broke out.

John Lovelo

Work for a blacksmith

Westinghouse used to come up for odds an ends, but mostly our work was with counci and electric people and things like the Wate Board. And another regular was the Catt Market. The Cattle Market was down by th Neeld Hall, 'side the river there, every Frida So we went in every Thursday just to see i alright, 'cause occasionally gates came off they'd get bent and broke and there was alwa something to do Fridays. For years we dor the Cattle Market and then, when it move up to Cocklebury later on, we still carried o maintenance and that. We used to do work fe the Tan Yard and places like that, they we always breaking things.

And just opposite us down Gladstone Roa there was the National Bus garage, a big o corrugated iron shed, part of Angel Hotel no but that was a bus garage in there. In thos days, of course, horses were just going ou and the cars coming in and tractors. We use to make tow bars to go on the car, the farm wanted to tow a trailer, 'cause he'd bring h milk into Nestlé's, and you couldn't go an buy tow bars in them days, so you had to s down and study a bit and make one up.

In those days, in the 1940s, we still bonde one or two wheels, you know, shrunk th iron bonds onto the wooden wheels. We ha bonding table out in the yard and that was quite a caper.

John Goodway

Work as a ticket girl

It was the headmaster that seemed to get you the careers thing. You had a list of jobs ... you had this form to fill in to say what you'd like to do and then if nothing came up they gave you a list of what jobs they'd found was vacant. Anyway I said hairdressing, they came back to me and said there wasn't any but there was this job in the post office.

The actual exchange itself was an upstairs extension on the back of the building and you couldn't see it if you were looking at the house face full on. Down the bottom was all the workings of the telephones and the actual exchange was up above. I started as what they call a ticket girl and that was collecting all the tickets that were made out when telephone calls came in. They had to be collected and sorted out, make the pots of tea when they wanted them and be a general dogsbody. It was £1 4s 6d a week and I thought, this'll be the job for me! The process with the tickets – well you had some pads of tickets, hundred and fifty on a pad. And you had to write down on the top where the call was going to, underneath where it was coming from, the time you'd connected the call and then the time they came off. And that would give the amount of minutes that they were talking and that's what they were charged for. But you had different rates – long distance, local, timed and untimed. I had to sort these tickets out and then they went into a big blue bag, which was tied at the top with a big string – like a drawstring bag and always had this leather label on. It had an address, but on my way home I always had to take it down to the sorting office. I done two years on the tickets and then at sixteen you were old enough to go

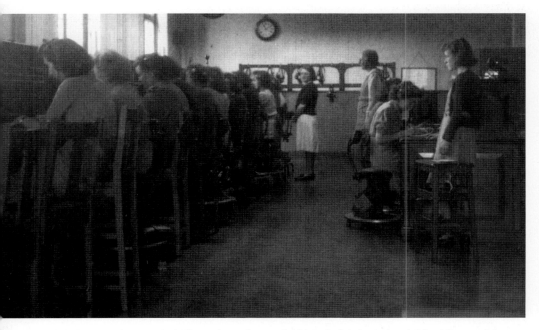

Chippenham telephone exchange, 1946. Pictured standing are Sybil Lovelock (*née* Jackson), Miss Milner and Jean Brind (*née* Miller) aged fourteen working as a ticket girl.

on to the telephones. I had to go to Bristol for six weeks and train down there and then come back to Chippenham, have two weeks supervision and then I was qualified as a telephone operator. When I first started, I think there was twelve what they call 'positions'. Each girl was on a position, with the dials and all the plugs and things on the front. But when I left in '57 there was twenty and they was nearly always manned, you know most of them manned. It was quite busy.

Then I was trained to be a supervisor, but it was too boring for me just standing up watching all of the work, unless there was any complications you had to get involved in. Too boring for me, so I asked to come off it and went on the phones again. The boss was a Miss Doris Milner. She was very, very nice, and worked alongside another under-supervisor named Joyce Edwards.

Jean Brind

The Telephone Exchange

I had a friend who worked at the telegram but I couldn't get in there, but I heard the were asking for telephonists. So I went fo an interview, got established and stayed fo twenty-two years! I saw it change very much with the telephones, because you used to hav to connect people to many, many places. Ther was a lot of manual exchanges around as wel Some had to come into us to get their calls. used to go out on these manual exchanges. got to know them very well. It was Hawthorn Devizes, I went to Box and Melksham. I sup pose there were about five different switch boards I could work. I was with my son man years later up at London in the museum, whe there was a switchboard there and he sai 'Mum, can you work that?', and I said 'Yes! so I was telling him, and when I looked roun there was crowds of people listening to me!

Shirley Ritchen

Manning the positions at the telephone exchange in the early 1950s.

n operator-assisted call

those days to make a call you'd pick up the
one and dial zero for the operator. Then
u'd have to put your money in or later
you had to put your money in to get the
erator. Then you only had so long, it was
timed precisely, you had to put the money
. You had to have the right money – it was
nnies and sixpences and what we call five
d ten p's now – shillings! As they put the
oney in the box you could tell what they'd
t in by the sound of the money going, they
ake little noises that I can remember, they'd
y and diddle you some of them! So you'd ask
em to press button B and get your money
ck and start again, because once they'd put
me money in they couldn't hear you – no
u couldn't hear them! Until they put the full
ount of money in and then you'd connect
em. I think I've got it right! It's amazing
ally, you can't sort of imagine – I mean there
as a lot of phone boxes, because not many
ople had telephones at home.

Sybil Lovelock

aining for the GPO

decided to join the GPO – the General
st Office – or Post Office Telephones. I
anted to be an engineer, although I never
ok apprenticeship. My father was with the
PO for a good many years and he was out
tting up the poles and so on and so forth.
hat's basically what I started with, because
u start from the menial things and you work
ur way up. So I started on the gangs, putting
the poles – going various places all around
d I then thought I would like to go onto
ting courses, within the company. I did that,
I was fitting telephones and extensions in
ople's houses. I decided that I should like
go a bit further, so I went on various other
urses. I did some City and Guilds courses to
with GPO as it was and then they decided

that they would change from the Crown to a
Public Corporation. It was known as British
Telecommunications. I got a position working
in the telephone exchange, maintaining the
equipment in the telephone exchange. It was
very different to what it is today.

Derek Brinkworth

The United Dairies

In 1968 I joined United Dairies. I remember
us all working there and, I'm not kidding, that
was very hard work, because you see we had
to stand. Well we weren't filling the bottles, the
machine was, but we had to take the bottles
off, put the bottles on. We were putting them
on to be washed and they go through the
machine and they come back the other side
filled with milk and then they went along a
conveyor belt. It was on Cocklebury Road,
about half way up. I worked there for a year
with them. That was hard work, but we used
to have a break, you know and have a chat.

Lucille Williams

A job and a half

I was a lad porter down the goods department
at the station. I used to make out consignment
notes and what we call taking the numbers of
all the wagons in the yard. I used to have to
go round all the sidings taking the numbers
of wagons and who they were for. There was
two signal boxes on Chippenham station –
Chippenham East and Chippenham West – and
there was also Langley Burrell, they had a signal
box there. I used to go across to Westinghouse
and take the numbers there. They had a siding
themselves, the bacon factory had a siding
– used to look after all that. Fancy going round
with a book that big, turning over the pages
like that – with an umbrella and trying to write
down! It was a job and a half, it really was.

Brian Tinson

Brian Tinson, left, receiving his twenty-five year service award from Unigate Dairies in 1976.

Office work

I went to work at the Co-op, in the offices. I was the filing clerk there for a while and then one of the girls, well she was going to come to the other office and they wanted someone to go where she was, which was in the telephone exchange – which was in the shop. The offices were in Foghamshire and the shop was in the High Street. So I had to transfer myself to the telephone exchange, learn how to do the telephone and everything. Also the vans that used to go out with bread and milk and everything, they used to come in to me and the men used to pay with all their tokens and money and everything and I used to have to check it all up. So that was really what I used to do. Apart from the time I used to vanish up into the cash office and help up there. Until the manager used to shout his head off, I won't repeat what he used to say, 'Where is

she again?', you know. So then I used to ha[ve] to come down into the office and eventua[lly] they did move the telephone exchange in[to] what they called the warehouse, so that the[re] were several girls in there. And I was just l[eft] with the books, with the men paying in a[nd] everything. The girl upstairs left – in the ca[sh] office – the one in the credit office went [up] to the cash office, so I went into the cre[dit] office. But they expected me to do the oth[er] job as well, with the tokens and the boo[ks] and everything. I used to change the boo[ks] over, it was – if you remember, you used [to] have a number. Everyone had a number [at] the Co-op – everything that was bought, y[ou] put against the number and I used to ha[ve] to change the books over every day, becau[se] obviously they had to be checked up a[nd] everything and I refused to do the two jo[bs] so I got the sack! I did leave on my own, b[ut]

taff of the Co-op bakery, pre-1920.

when I come in he – Bennett – said to me 'What are you doing here?' I said 'I'm working my notice'. 'No need, you can clear off'. And then I went to Westinghouse to work. And they were the happiest days of my life. I often think why did I stay at the Co-op? It was much nicer at Westinghouse than it was at the Co-op. Thinking about it, I think I was stupid to stay there so long.

Peggy Chamberlain

Doing National Service

I had to do National Service. I went into the Army with the view of gaining – I would have liked to have learnt something about the radio trade or you know – communications or driving skills, mechanical engineering, that sort of thing, and so I put down on the form – the REME, various other groups that I would like to go into, and when it came I had to report to the RA. The RA – I thought what the heck's the RA? I remember getting on the train at Chippenham and this chap said 'I'm going to the Royal Artillery'. I said 'I don't know about that, I'm going to the RA'! The penny hadn't dropped that it was the same! I started off in Oswestry. I must have been in my twenties as opposed to eighteen, because I'd been to university. All these chaps, I suppose they were NCO's, warrant officers and the like, and they had sticks, huge sticks, all yelling and bawling – and all these sort of horrible looking civvies got off the train. Anyway I soon came to the conclusion that the Army wasn't going to do for me what I was hoping. You know, I thought I would benefit. I mean, there was very little application for artillery work in Civvy Street!

Michael Gee

Delivering the milk for the Chippenham Dairies, c. 1900.

Work at the Co-op

When I went to the Co-op I sort of did everything. Well I did everything during the war,
except deliver coal! I delivered milk, I delivered
bread and, of course, we had no men. You had
to unload lorries and all that sort of thing and
weigh things up in the little blue bags or else
you had to make a triangle thing and fold it up
and put things in there. That was all put in great
big old tin baths. Your sultanas and everything.
You'd weigh them up with the scoop and fold it
down and weigh it. And I chopped chops, let me
tell you, in the butcher's shop! And things like
that! Oh yes I was in the butcher's shop in the
Co-op and remember selling whale meat during
the war. And at Christmas time we had all the
chickens and things and I used to help pluck
the chickens. You wore an overall – a white one
in the confectioner's but in the butcher's shop,
when I did things like that, I had a green one.

Margaret Smith

Hearing tests

I went to work for the Trowbridge Healt
Department in Trowbridge. As an audiome
trician, which was a fairly new service then.
went around the school with a clerk, testin
all the children's hearing. I usually started o
with the infants, the reception class, whic
was very interesting, because anything that
noticed I made a note of when I was testin
their ears and we did manage to pick up a lo
of different things. There were baby clinic
then and they did pick up most of the thing
with the children and I stayed there work
ing for schools, doing clinics for the hospita
– the ENT Department at Chippenham an
Swindon. We did clinics out in Highwort
and Wootton Bassett, Corsham. All the outly
ing villages.

Sybil Lovelo

aff at Nestlè's factory in the early 1930s.

arm work

/ell I was fifteen years old when I left school
id the intention was that I would become an
prentice agricultural engineer, but as there
ere no vacancies at that time, the school
aving officer advised that I should work on
farm. So I actually got a position living in at
ower Hanger Farm at Bremhill. It was quite
rict and I used to be the one who had to
t up early in the morning, get the cows in
id I'd be there till late at night to put the
ens in when they went to bed and all this
ind of thing. And I weren't at all happy. So I
:tually left then, came back to Chippenham
id I found employment with Farmer Poole,
ho farmed Lower Farm, Hardenhuish. And
was very happy there. It was a really old-
shioned farm, there was no tractors, there
as just horses and I got on well with horses
id the rest of the animals, in fact, I particu-
rly liked the horses and worked quite a lot

with them. And I used to drive the milk float,
bring that into Chippenham with the milk on
for Nestlé's every morning and then pick up
things to take back to the farm. There was also
an old oil merchant by the name of Tommy
Rose – he had a horse-drawn oil cart and he
had an old ex-Army horse and sometimes that
horse wasn't well. So the horse that I used with
the milk float, we used to put in the oil cart
and I used to have to go round with him to
Chippenham, to Yatton Keynell, Kington St
Michael and then back again. So my early days
were quite interesting. Anyway, following that,
as no work came forward for an apprentice
agricultural engineer, the second choice was to
be a carpenter and, although I was by this time
just on sixteen, I was apprenticed to Hulbert-
Light in Chippenham as a carpenter-joiner.

Alan Horner

The staff of Woolworths pictured with manager Mr Dawson, shortly after its opening in 1932/33.

The Southern Electricity Board

My mother used to collect a pension from the Electricity Board and Mr Webb, who was the manager then, said 'There's a job if your daughter would like to come and work here?' My father had worked for the Electricity Board and mother always hoped I'd be a demonstrator – they had demonstrators in those days of cookers and things like that, and I'd done very well in cookery. I'd got a distinction for cookery at school and she thought I would perhaps be interested in that. Anyway I settled in at the Electricity Board as a junior, answering phones, making tea and all that sort of thing. Then at the same time as I

was taking exams – it must have been abou the last year at school I suppose – a frien decided she would like to do shorthand an typing. Would I join her? So I took the fir exam there and I was also doing what w the equivalent to A Levels. It was called th Certificate and I don't think you are prob ably allowed to do that now. And then I wer for the Electricity Board in Chippenhar and went on and took advanced shorthan and typing. Because the pay was NALG [National Association of Local Governmer Officers], you got paid according to you exam results.

Doris Roddha

four

Westinghouse Brake and Signal Company

Aerial photograph of the Westinghouse works in the 1950s, showing the terraced housing of Hawthorn and Tugela Roads on the left.

A lifetime's work

My father worked all his life at Westinghouse. He was a craftsman, what was known as a sheet metal worker. Later on – when I was at Westinghouse – I got allocated to his department, which was a proud moment for him ... I'm not so sure what it was for me! My father was pretty steady. Same job all his life. My mother, when she married, did not work at all, as happened in those days. So she was the traditional housewife. Lunchtimes my dad would cycle home for his lunch, in the hour that he had. Back to work and very traditional sort of life. Straight down the middle was my dad.

Tony Knee

Engraving gun sights

My first job was when I went to Westinghou in the April when I left school. And I was packer, I used to pack the units, but after th I went on an engraving machine and I w on that for all the time then. Unless they g short of work and we were put somewhe else, but I used to work in an office then. B really I was doing engraving. I was eightee when the war started and I worked ten yea at Westinghouse on ammunitions. So I had reserved occupation. Before the war started, was in the rectifier shop. But we used to c engraving, a lot of brass plates, name plates, a that type of thing. We was also engraving c bakelite, and things like that, you know.

Mr William Young (left), Ivy Ward's father, pictured working at Westinghouse.

I really wanted to get away from it altogether. But, of course you couldn't, I mean you couldn't leave a job during the war. You had to stay there. I used to go up to the college evenings, I was learning typewriting and shorthand and that at college at night. That was when I won this sort of Westinghouse prize, I won a nice handbag for the best student at college. It was organised by Westinghouse. It was sort of like an apprenticeship thing.

Freda Curtis

A five year apprenticeship

After my schooling in Bath, I took an apprenticeship at Westinghouse. While waiting to start the apprenticeship I worked at Nestlé's for about six weeks. I was just making up boxes and helping packing and doing odd jobs down there, when they used to do the condensed milk in those days. Then I went to Westinghouse and done a five-years electrical testing-fitter apprenticeship. There was several hundred of us altogether. We used to do four days a week at the works – Westinghouse – and one day a week at college, which I always found hard. I found it hard to pass my exams. It was a very good apprenticeship because you started off at the place where you would eventually finish up – which for me was the electrical test rooms. Then you go through all the various departments. You went through the machine shop, the foundry, the fitting shops – various fitting shops – the laboratory and all that. You do the last twelve months there and then you are automatically taken on in that department. Finally I worked at Westinghouse for three years in the rectifier department and the Westerlite department and things got a little bit difficult there with redundancies and I decided to make a move.

Don Little

Working on the rectifiers

I was in the rectifiers at Westinghouse. And then I moved over to testing transformers. And I stayed in there until I retired. A rectifier changed alternating, like we got now, to direct [electrical current] and the equipment was mainly, depending on what size you did, for supplying the electricity to plating vats. Of course they used to make these up, they were great big things, they would either be one, two, three or four units with a big fan on the top and all joined up with big copper bars all the way along.

Norman Beazer

Working a Burrough's machine

When it came to me leaving school, I went off to Westinghouse and I don't quite know how I got it, but I got on the staff. I was in the cost office. Dad, in his wisdom, bought me a typewriter, 'cause I thought I'd like one. And I told them when I went to the job that I could type and I got the job as a typist in the cost office. Soon found I couldn't type! So I was given a card with the proper way to type on and told that I would be sent to school once a week to learn. Unfortunately that fell through and I never did go to school, but I did learn to type properly. I stayed there as a typist for a while, about eighteen months,

and by this time the war was on and I wa called into the head's office and he said, 'We'r moving you' because the men were all goin to war. So he said, 'You are going to the Section', and I was put on a section wit some old men, which I didn't like. So I wer back as a typist for a couple of weeks an then was put on the E Section and there wa some younger men there and I stayed ther Thoroughly enjoyed that one actually, becaus I knew what I was doing. It was things that could recognise because we were in the co office and the things that I was costing, th E Section, was all the electrical section and could understand it.

And I was doing very well there, but wasn't too long before I was back into th head's office again and he said, 'We're ver short on the Burroughs machines and we'r going to transfer you there'. You were a typis and a Burroughs machine was a typing an adding machine – I suppose an early forr of computer really, because as you type i the figures on the columns of cost sheets, s they added them up. It was ever so cleve But if you pressed two keys together there tremendous noise and the whole office cam to a stop. So I was put on these Burrough machines and that was with all women.

Ivy Ward

Assembly work

I decided that I wanted to move on, so got a job with Westinghouse and I worke in the rectifier assembly department. I wa working mainly in the stores, getting nuts an bolts, things, whatever people needed on th benches. There was mainly a hundred wome working in the shop, there was only abou a dozen men, so we had to keep the ladie happy supplying what they needed. They wer on piece work.

Derek Brinkwortl

Office staff at Westinghouse celebrate Christmas, 1933. Mr H.A. Cruse, Director and Works Manager, is seated centre.

The lighter side of rectifiers!

I worked in the Tax Office for a time and then I was jacked up to Westinghouse as soon as the war started. I went up there absolutely furious, I wasn't going to be there – ended up I was there for thirty-three years! Did a lot of work for the Admiralty and the Air Ministry and Post Office. Did a lot of work for submarines here. Well I was in the department for the rectifiers. I think they made the equipment to go in the submarines and power stations. We did some for Drax and various power stations, but they were great big machines – about a thousand volts to run and what they did we never knew! Parts of the aeroplanes. Rectifiers were a big thing in those days. The part I worked in – the rectifiers – was fairly clean. Not too far really from the fresh air – I was going to say! In

the machine shop or the furnace shop – any of those, you had the horrible thick atmosphere. Our shop backed onto the railway line, so we had the windows open. They employed quite a lot of girls there, but they were on the lighter side of rectifiers. They were upstairs and downstairs – I was in the office with the heavy machinery tests and things. Miles of typing – these Ministry forms. The Admiralty they had copy – seven sheets to it! D55s, and you typed those, you make a mistake on the first sheet … and of course the men used to write pages, very long figures – keep all the figures of tests and such. They all had to be typed, well nowadays they just go into a copier and that would be that! Now we had to do five or six copies – seven for the Admiralty, you daren't make a mistake.

The Stamp Shop at Westinghouse 1950. This photograph was taken just moments after the two-ton tup had hit the white hot metal.

Carbon paper was filthy. I think they were D40s, I think they were about seven copies. I know they were a lot. Post Office weren't quite as bad, but the Admiralty and the Air Ministry were about the worst work.

Elizabeth Perrett

Working in payroll

I left school at fifteen in August 1955 and I managed to get a job in an office in Westinghouse. Working on Powell Farmers machines. Very huge, huge typewriters. Probably five or six feet high and all the things along the front like one extended long typewriter of letters and numbers and very wide sheets of paper, eighteen inches wide – the roll of paper. You fed the paper in around the roller, just like a typewriter and we made out the payslips every week for the six thousand people that worked in Westinghouse. We even did them for the London payroll, because they had some office staff who were stationed and working in London for quite a long time and we used to do their payslips as well. They had to be done, no matter what the machine threw up at you and how many wobblers it threw, they had to be finished by Thursday evening and be down in the cashier's office. So Thursday evenings I never knew quite what time I was going home.

I worked there for twelve years, sort of advancing up and being given more and more responsibility. Then during that time they actually built a purpose-built building for the new computer. They would laugh at us now – when they look at a laptop! – because the new computer, back in the late fifties or early sixties, would have more than filled my lounge! Huge, huge piece of equipment, right in the middle of the room, with all these metal doors that lifted off to see the menagerie of wires behind it. We had engineers on site all the time to see to them if they went wrong or any of our machines started playing up. I mean we had machines that would first of all reproduce exactly the card you'd got, for exactly the same again – the repeat of it. You had one machine that you put them in and it would print along the top edge all the information that was punched there. Then you would have machines that would sort them into different operations and you've probably seen those on the television where they come down into little angled slots, all along and they're sorted and whatever. Then you've got the tabulator where they would go together, they would mix and merge them together. It would take one from here and three from there and one from here and three from there and mix them in together and sort them. In the next door oom was a punch room, where they punched he cards in the first place. Sometimes if they vere struggling, my boss Mr Mortimer'd say o me 'Marian would you like to go in the punch room and help us out?' and I would go n and help punch the cards and then come pack and put them all through the other processes anyway.

Marian Stickland

Redundancy

You probably remember that in the sixties here was a certain Dr Beeching around. Now Dr Beeching was told to prune the railways. There was me – I was a railways signalling engineer – and what happened was nearly all of us ex-apprentices were made redundant. I guess it would be 1963? So we weren't singled out – it was en bloc. Somebody had to go, so we had very polite letters saying that we were not going to get these signalling contracts and there wasn't much happening elsewhere n the world and having only just started my ob it was almost inevitable that we would go. So off we go… I was fortunate because I got a job immediately. Within about six months I was asked if I would like to return to Westinghouse, there was a vacancy, and Robert Methuen – he had been my boss previously – and my father met me off the train and explained the position to me. So very quickly I was production engineer on the shop floor as a go-between, between design and production. Also I was on the electrical side in the rectifier division. So I'd gone from railway signalling to rectifier division. This was heavy electrical stuff and I quite enjoyed it.

Tony Knee

Watch out for the bikes!

The bikes were the one for Westinghouse. You had to stand clear at the end of Foundry Lane when they all came out for lunch at twelve o'clock, because about six thousand bikes would just take over the road and you'd better stand back! Then they would trickle back in from ten to one onwards, so you just avoided that and when they came home at five o'clock at night or whatever you'd get out of the way again! Our house backed onto Westinghouse. We were quite used to the bikes and Westinghouse and the sounds of the factory around us.

Marian Stickland

Working for the Ministry

The reason why we came down here was because of my father – he'd been trained by the Ministry, and he was working at Kemble when war broke out. He was in digs in Cirencester, travelling from Cirencester to Kemble and then he went to work at Hullavington and then he moved into digs in Chippenham. I don't know where he lived. I know my mother, when we were actually bombed out of London, she moved into Greenway Lane. Then we ended up in Ladyfield Road and my father carried on working at the Ministry till around about '47 and then they had the opportunity to leave and he went to work for Vickers Armstrong over Keevil, Trowbridge way. He was there for five years or so, then he went to work at Westinghouse and he worked there for ten years. He was made redundant in the sixties and there wasn't no work suitable for him round here, and he actually moved back up to London. Took digs and lived away from Ladyfield Road and he was up there for the last twelve years of his working life. Just come home weekends. There was no chance of getting re-housed up in London. He did make enquiries, but there was just no chance.

Then I went to work at Westinghouse when I left school in '54, when I was fifteen.

Norman Stacey

Employees at Westinghouse leaving via the Hawthorn Road gate in the early 1950s.

five

The War
Years

'God help us all'

I can remember sitting listening to the radio – and I can remember my mum saying, 'God help us all!' I can remember her saying that. And the air-raid sirens went that night then, for the first time, but they said it was just a practice...

Margaret Smith

The day war broke out

The morning when the war started, Mr Churchill was on the radio, said the war was started at eleven o'clock. About a quarter of an hour afterwards the police was all round the streets, shouting out 'Will everybody go down to Ladyfield', there was no houses there then, they was just started building them and 'Would we all go down there and fill sand-bags'. We were down there all day, filling these sandbags, well there was hundreds down there doing them and they had these carts to take them away, but the next morning, oh, you oughta saw my hands. The next thing they were all put up on the bridge, round by the Neeld Hall, and up the town. Years later they were still there and you go up the town and there're all weeds coming out, it was so funny to see all the weeds and the grass and flowers and all, but it was really the foundations they were getting up for these houses. Well we had some laughs at times.

Freda Curtis

Preparations for war

I was only twelve when the war broke out and we were roped into various things. By September my mother was already involved in preparations for the evacuees. She was up a

The Chippenham Home Guard Band, led by Harry Havenand, pictured outside the Ivy.

the Secondary School at Cocklebury serving food and tea and working with allocations and working out where evacuees had to go and from then on we were all swept up into wartime activities. Then they opened a canteen in Foghamshire, before the NAAFI came in, and we kids were involved in helping with that as there was a kitchen. In the canteen itself there were things to entertain the troops – pianos, books, billiard tables upstairs and somebody had to run up and down with trays of food so that was a useful thing for us children.

Avice Wilson

The blackout

The war years – they were dark, they were dismal, but people were friendly, we had some good times. Bearing in mind that I lived about two miles out at Sheldon Corner – I had to cycle everywhere. It was blackout, you had a cycle light, but your beam had to be going down and my dad ran a car still. Looking back we were very, very fortunate as a family, because we had a car. But the cars, they had shields put on with slots in. Going to Sheldon Corner there was no street lights and after great-gran's house there was what we called the back-to-front house, which is by Lowden's church now, then there was Pipsmore Farm and cottages, then there was nothing else to Sheldon Corner. So it was very sparse, very dark.

Ivy Ward

Decorating the blackouts

My very earliest memories are, I think, sitting on the stairs with a candle, with mum and my baby brother, as aeroplanes went over. Our staircase was the only place in the house that had no window in it. Mum was on her own at that time because my dad had been called up. We just had this strange man come home every so often in uniform to see us – and it was always my dad! I was born in the middle of the war, 1941. I can remember him away. I can remember the blackout curtains, mum used to decorate the inside of the blackout curtains. She was quite good at handicrafts and what not. And stenciling was quite a thing of hers and she used to decorate the inside, so that when they were down at night she didn't have to draw the curtains then, but she had something pretty to look at.

Peggy Burgess

Disturbed nights

During the war years, we actually shared the house with a very old gentleman. He had a room upstairs and a room down and we had the rest of the house. I can remember the air-raid shelter, just outside our house in the middle of the road. Luckily there weren't the cars that there are today. I can remember gas masks and having younger sisters and brothers, I can remember the baby one was kept in the cupboard under the stairs, in case the baby needed it. It was an entire thing. It was like putting a baby into a 'babygro' of rubber, with the mask at the top of it.

When we were at school, we had to go to bed in the afternoon for a little while because of disturbed sleep at night and we had little wooden beds and we had a pillow that we kept and hung up on a hook in what would be like a 'dap bag'. We'd go and fetch our pillow and lay down for a little while after lunch. We were also given orange juice to drink. We were given bottles of milk – a third of a pint of milk every day and we had to queue up to get our spoonful of cod liver oil – urgh!

Margaret Smith

Incendiary bombs

We were on line for all the big bombing raids to the Midlands and when they blitzed

Birmingham, Coventry and that I remember all night long the throbbing of aircraft overhead. And of course when they hit Bath, we saw the glow in the sky. The only instance that I remember action – they dropped some bombs up at the Folly crossroads and someone was in the bath up there and the ceiling came down on them!

German planes used to bomb the harvest fields in summer and we children used to go out on our bikes and collect the fins of the incendiary bombs. These were steel or some metal that didn't burn. We used to come back with carriers full of them on our bikes! Just collect them! I suppose they all disappeared eventually.

David Hall

Waste paper collection

In the early part of the war I was with the 1st Chippenham Scouts in Audley Road. At the beginning of the war, we started collecting waste paper and we used to go round different areas of town every Saturday morning and afternoon to collect waste paper, and we stored and sorted it at the old mill, Monkton Hill. But unfortunately we had a fire there and put an end to that activity!

Frank White

Listening to the news

The radio was a big thing in those days. During the war the news was a big thing, to see what was happening. My father came from Sheffield and my mother came from Gravesend and both those areas were bombed during the war. quite severely, and I suppose, with hindsight, it was important to them to know what was going on. My mother's father was still living in Gravesend. Perhaps my grandmother as well, but the great part of the war it was just my grandfather down in Gravesend. My father had two sisters up in Sheffield and various

British soldiers stationed at the Catholic Hall, pictured in St Mary's Place at the back of the Palace, pose with local children.

other relations, and well they both must have been very concerned. And so silence had to prevail – 'The news – shut up!'. It was quite incredible, so I've inherited that yen to hear the news!

Michael Gee

Keeping the radios going

My father, Stanley Alves, had been working for Bulson's, which was in Park Lane then. As the war approached, like everybody, we were listening to the radio and what was going on, how the Germans were occupying things and father said 'Something's going to happen'. And he said to Bulson's 'I think we should get into the store things that are important to radios, to keep radios going. I know exactly what could go wrong'. So they said 'Do what you like!' so he did and we had our house, their house, the shop – full of stuff for him to repair the radios. And it paid off, because he was the only one in the whole district that could repair the radios. When he was the right age for being called up, I think he was about thirty-four then, he went and they said 'What do you do?' And he said 'I repair the radios. All my staff have gone. I'm only left'. So he got exempt. And he kept the whole of Chippenham and the district going right through the war with radios. There was all those people fighting and that's how father kept it going on the home front, so people could listen. Because that was most important for people to hear what was going on and hear Churchill and all of those people.

Shirley Ritchens

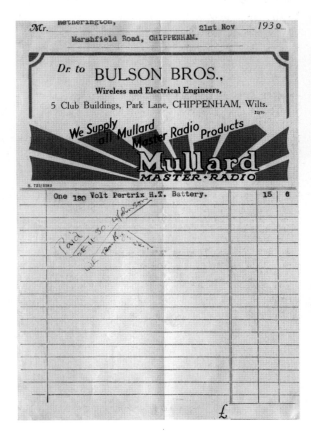

Letter heading for an invoice from Bulson Brothers, Park Lane, from 1930.

Women work on the assembly lines at Westinghouse during the war years.

Working on the ammunitions

Westinghouse went over then to ammunitions. And mostly, I was on gunsights. We had to do the lines and the numbers you know, on gunsights. All different sorts. We did the brass ones for the big guns. Then we used to do aluminium for the aeroplanes. Things like that. I was at Westinghouse ten years altogether and during the war. I finished up there in 1944. We had four engraving machines. The rest of the shop we were in was all men. But, the first time I went there, when I did the packing that was all ladies in that shop and I think just the bosses was men. I enjoyed that although really speaking, it weren't a job I wanted. Went on half past seven in the morning to half past seven at night. And half past seven at night to half past seven in the morning. All through the blackout. When the sirens went, we had to go up at the back and into these sort of dugouts in the ground at the back of Westinghouse.

Freda Curtis

Living to tell the tale

My husband was a plumber on Lyneham, laying the pipes under what became the airfield. They were quite used to planes coming round and landing, but this somehow sounded a little different, this one. He stopped and looked up from the trench he was down in and thought 'something different about that one'. The he saw that the bombs had been dropped and it was heading straight towards him and he was in front of hanger three. He was in the pipework in the ground … he stood there and watched and this bomb drifted over and it hit the next hangar – four – which was still in construction. If it had hit hangar three, he wouldn't have been there to tell the tale, and it would have taken about two hundred personnel who were working on the planes in the hangar that day. But because the circulation of the air had taken it over enough, it had hit hangar four, and there were only about four men who sadly lost their lives. Then, back in 2002, we were invited to go to Lyneham airfield with a group of people. They entertained us and we had a film and we went and looked round the old Albert [Hercules aircraft] and then we had refreshments afterwards. But they made a little bit more of my husband that day, because he had been the only one who actually saw the bomb. They had never until that point found anyone, in the forty years, that had seen it happen and was still alive to tell the tale.

Marian Stickland

Preparing for the RAF

I didn't do the full five years apprenticeship because the war had started and I can remember saying to Mr Parks, 'I'm gonna be called up before very long and so would you mind if I leave early?' He agreed to it and I then went up to Colerne aerodrome. That was being built at the time. I went up there and was working as a joiner. All the hangars were built then, you know the mess huts part of it, but at the side of the hangars, we were putting up concrete shuttering for the concrete roads, you know. There wasn't a great deal of skill involved as regards carpentry-joinery work with it, but I mean you did anything then. War was on and you did what you were told to do. I remember the planes going over to bomb Bristol, that would have been 1940 I think. In fact when the hooter would go up there, you'd scarper over the edge of the airfield into the woods. I can remember one day they dropped one bomb on the aerodrome. They dropped it on what was the NAAFI. I mean even then the aerodrome wasn't built, wasn't finished then, put it that way. They were still building houses for the airmen and things, but the BAC [British Aircraft Corporation] took over the first two hangars, the dome-shaped hangars that were built. They were sending aeroplanes in there. Aircraft was coming from America in big crates you know. We used to use the crates, for shuttering for the concrete. It was a British base. I mean there were planes in the hangars we were working in. They were desperate for use of them I suppose. There was always planes in there – the Spitfires and the Lysanders, planes like that, you know. In fact they were operating from there the last few months of 1941, before I was called up, night fighters and things like that. There were no bombers there then.

John Lovelock

Stationed around Chippenham

Every Sunday afternoon I used to go down to what was the Toc H rooms down in Foghamshire and it was a forces canteen. I used to assist down there in bringing up sandwiches, cakes and things from down in the kitchen. Bringing them up to the counters to be served. There were camps everywhere.

Group of Chippenham ARP wardens, Sector C, pictured with their wives at the back of the old TA centre, Ivy Lane.

The main places were Hullavington, Lyneham, Compton Bassett and Yatesbury. Where else? There was a camp at Melksham. I don't think they had many people from there. Whenever you go round the country now, you say you're from Chippenham – quite a lot of people say 'Oh I remember that. I used to be stationed at Compton Bassett or Yatesbury'.

Frank White

Civil Defence

Civil Defence was a big thing. My father, he felt that he should partake in the affairs of the town and when the war started he became quite a live wire in the ARP – the Air-Raid Precaution. Everyone squeezed in a bit during

the war and we had a room which had been a garage by the original owners and that was used as an air-raid warden's post. Of course that meant we got a telephone, because the post had to have a telephone and so I was introduced to the luxuries of the telephone at a very early age! We didn't have a telephone prior to that and this thing – the telephone – was a marvel. My father, he used to go out – I don't know whether he was the chief warden, he used to go round to other air-raid warden posts within the town and he'd come back and he'd reek of smoking. He used to wear a Homburg at one time and an old black overcoat and he rode a bike, a very old sit up and beg bike with a basket on the front.

Michael Ge

ARP group at Birch Grove, Chippenham in 1941.

Joining the Home Guard

The sirens … there was one round on the Town Hall, there was one round at the Five Alls Inn – on the roof round there. Of course here was the Home Guard. I was about seventeen, eighteen, when I joined the Home Guard. We were up at the ambulance station then, before it was developed to what it is now. It was still like stables then, belonging to Hardenhuish House. There was a door outside of the house and a staircase you could get up. There was a bit of an old tower on the old house from memory, you could get up there and we used to walk all round Hardenhuish House, waiting for all the parachutists that were supposed to be going to drop. Goodness knows what would have happened if any of

them did! I don't know that we would have lasted five minutes really!

I think one of the fellows that was in charge was the engineer working down in Nestlé's. Also Mr Spinkes, you know Spinkes' printing works, I suppose he was either one of the sergeants or one of the officers. We did the usual rifle training, things like that. Went up to the firing range over Heddington. Other than that it was just the fact of doing your duty – one or two nights a week, or something like that we'd go up there and do two hours on, two hours off and then go back to work at eight o'clock the same morning! You didn't stay home from work because you were up all night, but we were all young then, plenty of energy I suppose!

John Lovelock

Civil Defence instruction

About 1939, I don't know how it came about, but Scouts have been renowned as messengers in emergencies. My name got put forward and a few weeks before the war I helped at the ARP department, Air-Raid Precaution, later to be called Civil Defence. That operated from a room in the police station in New Road. I remember going out on a number of occasions to different wardens. I remember cycling out to Bolehyde Manor at Allington and taking something out there in connection with this Air-Raid Warden service. Somehow or other, the police took over running the Civil Defence Section, a sergeant by the name of Sergeant Smyth, and I spent a lot of time in Chippenham police station in connection with the wardens, doing these message deliveries. This police sergeant was trained as a Civil Defence Instructor and he went on courses on poison gas. Remember we'd all been issued with gas masks by then. Later on, he went on a course on unexploded bombs and part of his job was to go round and lecture to wardens in different places; Chippenham, Corsham, Malmesbury and he raked me in for operating the slide projector! I remember going to several of these places and while he did the talking, I was operating the slides. Always were the same thing time and time again, but I'd say it was quite interesting and he used to keep me supplied with lemonade and pork pies. I was lucky – everybody else had their travelling curtailed with having taken their cars off the road. No petrol allowed. I was being driven around the countryside and seeing things I wouldn't have normally seen!

Frank White

Working with the Land Girls

By then the Land Girls were here and there was also the fact that the farmers' wives, would work on the farms sometimes. One of the things helped me was my physique because I was tall and large and fairly strong. So I adapted quite well, but then that's not really fair because we had little diminutive Land Girls that could do wonderful things. It was really remarkable the physical labour that the women did. I used to stand in awe at the threshing machine girls that used to come. They'd work all day handling the sheaves, it was a terribly dusty job and they would wear a mask over their face, or a handkerchief over their face, and they'd have their hair in a bandanna with their curlers in. Then they'd go back to their hostel and they would shower and they'd get the curlers out of their hair and they'd be at the local dance looking a million dollars, you know. It was amazing, and that was damned hard work that they used to do.

Avice Wilson

Testing the gas masks

There used to be a mobile gas chamber which used to be up in the Wharf. They used to fill it with gas and then all the children used to go up, put all the gas masks on and walk into this room – just to check what it was like to have a gasmask on and I suppose some way to prove that the gasmasks was working. Used to have to take these boxes, later on we had round tins with these gas masks in. They were horrible things. The rubber mask on you – pressing on you – and try and breathe … there were some better ones, I think with separate eye pieces and a tube from the mouth down on to a container on the body, but they weren't for the public. They were for the military or the police or something like that.

David Ha

Tank traps

I lived in Monkton Hill and just opposite where I lived, in St Mary's Place, there wa

vo or three families of children and we
ways used to play altogether. We used to
lay a lot up at the top of Station Hill on
 spare piece of ground, which was next to
he Chippenham GPO Sorting Office. I can
ways remember during the war, just by this
iece of ground there was a lot of concrete
ones. They were put there in the road to
op tanks going through if we were invaded
uring the war. They were really solid con-
ruction and the tanks couldn't get to the
ilway that way. The other side of the road
as a row of railwayman's cottages, there was
ese big concrete cones and then there was
is piece of spare ground. So a tank wouldn't
 able to get through at all to the railway.
hey would have to go up the Cocklebury
oad and I think there was some more forti-
ations further along to stop them getting to
e railway station.

Don Little

lore than enough gas masks!

 did fire watching because I was in St
hn's Ambulance. We had to come up to
estinghouse when the siren went. Not that
e ever done a great lot, but you just had to be
ere on watch. My husband was in the Home
uard, because he worked at Westinghouse
 a reserved occupation. When we first got
arried we had a bungalow and we had all
ese little cardboard gas masks. We had six
s masks between us – he had one for the
ome Guard, that was a big gas mask, the
her gas mask was a bit smaller which was for
eet watching, then he had this little one. I
d one for Westinghouse, that was a big one
d I had one with 'Warden' on, then we had
ır little ones. So we had six gas masks and
gun between us. We thought 'Where are we
ing to put them?' The only wall we could
ıt 'em all on was the bathroom, so that was
 with all the gas masks on. And I don't know

when we moved out what they thought of the
bathroom with all these hooks! It was sort of
funny really.

Freda Curtis

Digging for victory

A donkey was refugeed from Bristol, from
some costermonger, and he spent his war at
the Ivy in the orchard and we harnessed him
up into the trap, because the two gardeners
were kept on all through the war. There was
just three acres of productive kitchen garden
and the flower beds around the house grew
cabbages and things, all neatly planted in
patterns! Carrots or whatever the crop was.
All the war, vegetables were grown – and fruit
– and the produce was taken up the town and
sold to Banks, not Maurice Banks – the other
one. There were two Banks' greengrocer's in
the High Street. You used to supply them with
what one grew – produce – and the donkey
took them up and so on!

Susan Rooke

Wartime life

Evacuees were billeted all around the town
– in the laundry in London Road, most of
the public houses had them in their rooms.
Well I can remember we did have quite a lot
of air-raid sirens … if they were bombing the
north, we had lots of planes going over. And
I remember when they bombed Coventry
– that was going on all night long. And my
mother used to make me get up and sit under
the stairs. Well my mum and dad used to make
home-made wine and you'd be sat there and
all of a sudden there was this explosion and
it was the corks coming out the wine bottles!
The tanks used to rattle through the town
a lot. I can remember the tank traps on the
Bridge and they had one in between Burton's,
didn't they. When I was in the Co-op, when

Display at Westinghouse of items produced for war use.

the plane machine-gunned Town Bridge, we had a fellow that was supposed to warn us. There was like a dome on the top of the Co-op, he'd go up there and if any enemy plane came within sight, he was supposed to ring a bell for us all to go out. Anyway I heard this crack, crack, crack and there was a bus going by – I thought 'Oh the bus is backfiring'. Anyway the bell went and I wondered what it was and then afterwards we were told that a plane – a German plane – had machine-gunned Town Bridge, but no-one was hurt. But that poor fellow never lived it down, because he rang the bell too late!

Margaret Smith

Called up – to Trowbridge!

I was desperate to get into flying crew. I we to Bristol. Had the medical – passed that ar thought 'I'm in now!'. And they said, 'You in a reserved occupation, you're working c an aerodrome'. So I didn't get into the RA Then at the end of '41, I was called up, in the Army, the Royal Corps of Signals. We a long way away – went to Trowbridge! Th barracks was there at Trowbridge. I rememb they sat us down in a classroom, stuck a pa of earphones onto us and said 'Right, no just try and see if you can tell the diffe ence between the different symbols'. We d a sixteen–eighteen week course, apart fro a bit of the square-bashing. It was basica learning Morse code and learning to be a

perator, which was quite interesting. I mean
ou sat there all day long bashing Morse, until
ou didn't know which way you were facing!
´ you didn't make the grade as an operator,
ien you went off into other things, perhaps
 dispatch rider or anything like that. Well, I
ought if I was going to have to stay in the
rmy I might as well have something interest-
g to do.

John Lovelock

vacuees from Hastings
about '41, they brought a lot of evacuees
om Hastings here. We had quite a big house
d my father was helping at the recep-
on centre, at what is now the Chippenham
ollege in Cocklebury Road. He came home
ne night with a lady with two young children
 stay with us for a year, eighteen months. Her
usband was still back in Hastings, but we had
telegram to say he'd been bombed out, could
 come down? – so he came down as well. He
ot a job out at RAF Hullavington, but shortly
ter that they were found some other accom-
odation, so we were back just to the family.
As far as I'm aware we got on with them
uite well. I believe there's one or two still
ving in this area. There were also a few
eople from the Channel Islands, 'cause as
ou know the Channel Islands were occupied
 the Germans and half the population were
vacuated and quite a number came into the
hippenham area. One of our school teachers
as a teacher come over from the Channel
lands.

Frank White

lot of extra work
think the evacuees would have been about
940/41. I remember my mother had billeted
 her two boys from Wanstead High School.
rst of all she had the older boy and then

later the younger boy, then after that she had
a family. The mother and two children. Their
name was Mason, I think. It was a lot of work
for my mother, I can remember that. The husband of the woman was in the RAF and she
didn't reckon to do much work, I don't think.
So it devolved upon my mother to look after
myself and her and her two children. I think
there was soldiers at Thingley, and I think they
used to come for a bath during the wartime! I
can't remember very much about it, but I can
remember that.

Doris Roddham

Billetted in Chippenham
I came to Chippenham in 1941, as a baby, eighteen to twenty months old with my mother;
we were billeted on a lady in Greenway Lane
and we were there for a few months and then
we moved into what would be our own house,
our own council house in Ladyfield Road. My
mother lived there until she died a few years
ago. She lived there for over fifty years.

Norman Stacey

The Yanks are coming!
Well I think the Americans must have come
overnight, because one day there was no-one
and then the next day well… I'll tell you the
story first of all … we had a dog and I used to
take the dog for a walk. And we've got a little
place up in Wood Lane we used to call Bull's
Hill. You went down and then there was a
little curve and it went down again in another
curve. Well I went round the second curve and
I stopped, because there was four soldiers there
in uniform and they had round hats on! So I
took one look and I went dashing back home
and I said 'Mam, there's Germans in Bull's
Hill!' Because I'd never seen an American
before – I thought they were Germans!

Margaret Smith

WESTINGHOUSE BRAKE & SIGNAL COMPANY LIMITED

· INLAND TELEGRAMS: ·
WESTINGHOUSE · CHIPPENHAM
WESTINGHOUSE · NORDO LONDON
· · TELEPHONES: · ·
CHIPPENHAM 2241 (4 LINES)
TERMINUS 6432 (10 LINES)

· · CABLES · ·
WESTINGHOUSE LONDON
· HEAD OFFICE ·
82, YORK WAY, KING'S CROSS
LONDON · N · 1 ·

CHIPPENHAM
WILTSHIRE

OUR REFERENCE	YOUR REFERENCE	DATE
HAC/TP/AEB.		9th January, 1945.

14600875 CFN. Gribble T.C.,
697 V.A.W. R.E.M.E.,
C.M.F.

Dear Gribble,

At this stage of the War, I feel it is desirable to write you personally as an employee of this Company prior to the 3rd. September 1939, to let you know that your War services to the Country have been appreciated by me and my colleagues responsible for the management of the Company.

At a recent meeting of the Principal Officers of the Company, at which Captain Peter, the Managing Director presided, it was decided that I should assure you that it is our intention, if you so desire, to reinstate you in the Company's employment in a position as favourable as is possible. Full consideration will be given to your wages, or salary, always bearing in mind the position you might have attained but for your period of War Service.

I feel you will welcome this reassurance as to your future with the Company, and it is our earnest hope that this letter will give you the satisfaction of knowing that you have not been forgotten. Everything possible will be done to see that your prospects will not be impaired by reason of your War Service, and every endeavour will be made to reinstate you in the Company's employment in a manner which will be satisfactory to you.

On behalf of myself and my colleagues of the Management, I send you our sincere good wishes.

Yours faithfully

WESTINGHOUSE BRAKE & SIGNAL Co., Ltd.

Director & Works Manager.

Letter from Westinghouse to Mr T. Gribble, confirming his re-instatement in 1945 after serving in the war.

nerican soldiers mix with local people at the British Legion Club before D-Day.

ijoying the war

/ell it's terrible really, but we enjoyed the war
 ars – because we were teenagers. You had
) responsibility whatsoever. I mean when
 think of mother – she must have been up
 le wall, trying to get enough for us to eat
 id everything, because of the rations. I can
 member we all gave up sugar, well except
 id and Jack, my brother, but the women
 d and it turned my dad grey, I know that
 he wasn't grey before the war, but he was
 ey when the war finished. By the time we
 ere nineteen, the Yanks arrived – the 4th
 rmoured Division, which was the cream of
 ie United States Army. And when the Yanks
 rived it was very nice actually!

Peggy Chamberlain

Making the Americans welcome

The first ones that came over didn't have a lot
to give us materially, we went to the dances
for the candy and everything, but we were also
there because we were noticed and they were
interested in us, whereas the British boys didn't
seem to be very interested. They used to come
into my father's shop on the slightest pretext
that they thought something was wrong with
their watch. They really came in because they
were fascinated by the little shop and just
maybe talk to people, because they were quite
lonely. Some of them were very lonely. Father
was hospitable and if they seemed interested
sometimes they would come home for a cup
of tea. I think of the times they were invited
to tea and seeing some of them trying to
balance the plate, teacup, where do they put
it, it must have been terribly confusing. Of
course they were entirely different from us but

a lot of them were still rural boys. It seemed to me that the first lot anyway, from the 2nd Armoured Division, were quite different from any idea of American boys that we may have had before.

Avice Wilson

Chewing gum

The Americans — we did see them at Sherston. But not a lot, only just sort of passing when they'd go through the village, when they used to give us kids loads of gum. There was a camp, just at Easton Grey — between Sherston and Malmesbury and they used to use our road quite a lot going up to Sherston to have a drink and what have you and meet up with the local girls. I mean I was only just a schoolgirl then, but they used to give us loads of gum. We always used to love it when we could see them coming up, they used to stop and say 'Would you like some gum?' And of course we would always say yes!

Jean Brind

An ease about them

There was the lack of class-consciousness with the Americans, they treated everybody the same. I was about fifteen with another school friend, walking past the Angel to go to the Gaumount cinema and an officer tried to pick us up and we were absolutely stunned! A British officer wouldn't look at two fifteen year olds let alone try and pick them up. We also met them at the dances at the Neeld Hall. I remember we were pre-pub age, so the other way we could meet was in the fish and chip line at Barrett's, that was great because if you didn't like them you could just walk away with your fish and chips and say 'Goodbye I've got to go home'. When we met them at the Neeld Hall it was just marvellous because you didn't sit for two minutes before you were

asked to dance. The British boys, they did dance very well anyway and they certain didn't jitterbug! The Americans had an ea about them. Then we had the 4th Armoure which was the one that stayed the long time. I think then it was the 82nd Infant came after that. That was after D-Day

Avice Wils

Which way to Chippenham?

I remember going for a cycle ride and th had taken all the signposts away … it was Je and I went actually, and she said 'Where sh we go?' and I said 'Well let's keep turning rig see where we get to' and we got lost! Becau there's no signposts, we didn't have a clue whe we were and in the end we saw this Ne Zealander and we said to him, 'Can you t us the way back to Chippenham please?' a he showed us. And I thought well fancy th — had to ask a New Zealander the way back Chippenham! We never lived that one down

Peggy Chamberla

Seeing the troops

I can remember going out for walks c a Sunday evening, which was always o thing in those days. We used to go down c the Town Bridge first of all, wait until t Salvation Army Band marched down throug the town to the Citadel. Then we used to g for a walk and I can remember particular going over the field towards Hardenhuis church, from the Malmesbury Road. On th right-hand side there was a big United Stat Army camp. There was also another big Arn camp — United States Army — as you go alon Hungerdown Lane, where Queen's Crescen is now and after they moved out it was th Chippenham United football ground. The even used one of the huts for changing i The other side of the road there was a Britis

orman Beazer and Lesley Ricketts at Henlow Camp,
ovember 1939.

nit, but they was down more behind the Bath
rch. There was a lot of lorries and tanks and
ings like that down there. I can remember
le old council offices in the Causeway – that
as an Army unit and I can remember one or
vo Army lorries up there as well. But they
ere all over Chippenham, stationed mostly
efore D-Day. We got quite friendly with a
w of the Americans. They used to get sweets
nd things like that and bring to us. They used
o come down to the houses, congregate with
s and we got very friendly with them.

There was a prisoner of war camp up the
nd of Greenaway Lane. I don't know whether
iey were Italians or Germans. There was a
ouse along Cocklebury Lane, they always
sed to say there was Italian prisoners of war

in there, but we never used to see anything.
But I can remember a camp at the end of
Greenway Lane – I don't know whether it
was pulled down or whether it's where St
Paul's School is now, but it was along there
somewhere.

Don Little

Italian POWs

The prisoners of war – we were very involved
with them at Cocklebury, being the nearest
farm to the town. First of all the Italians came
in gangs. It was sometime between 1942 and
'43. They worked out a system where they
had a local camp at Greenway Lane near
Bird's Marsh, the T-junction at the end of
Greenway Lane and Hill Corner Road. The
Italians could be trusted and so they would
walk to the local farms or would be taken by
bus daily to other farms further out. The ones
they could really trust were boarded at the
farms. We had two at Cocklebury – one of
them stayed until the end of the war. We got
very used to them. As the war wore on the
Italians had more and more privileges. They
were allowed to walk in the town, they wore
brown dyed battledress uniforms with a great
big coloured patch on the back. They were
always allowed to wear their regimental cap
on every Sunday when they were marched
into the Roman Catholic church. We used
to stop on our cycles and watch them go by;
eventually they were allowed in the town and
the cinema but never in the pubs.

Avice Wilson

Learning to jitterbug

We used to have a wonderful time really,
telephonists, because we used to get invited
to all the dances at all these places. They used
to send a truck at eight o'clock, when we all
finished, and we used to go dancing nearly

every night of the week. I learnt to jitterbug with the Americans in the Neeld Hall. They used to have dances in the Neeld Hall. Used to have dances in the Co-op Hall, which is now the Salvation Army and we used to go out to Corsham. They used to send what you might call a little Landrover for us then. Once we came back and the man said he was just going to drop us in the top of Chippenham. Well course, there was no buses anywhere and it was quite a long way to walk, but anyway we persuaded him to drop us all off at our different homes! We used to go for the food really. They served such wonderful spreads, specially if you went to some of the officers' places, they had even more food. I think we all seemed to be tired the next day, because we never used to get home until about three o'clock. It didn't stop us from going! They used to like having the telephonists, I think they probably thought we could talk!

Sybil Lovelock

Talking to dad

We used to have two Americans from the 4 Armoured come to my house. We used to dancing that sort of thing. My dad was an o soldier, he was a prisoner of war in the 19 to 1918 war, and of course he used to talk these boys and we used to hear things that never spoke to mum and me about, ever, ar we learnt more about his war with these tv boys being there, than we ever knew anythin about. But they were really nice boys, the really were – gentlemen really weren't th – and after they went, didn't bother with a more!

Margaret Sm

Prisoners of war

At the back of the house, the farmer used employ Italian prisoners of war. Ditching ar hedging at the back. A friend and I would g and visit at the farm and play with the Hawk

The Chippenham Sea Cadets Corps marching through Chippenham, having taken receipt of their new uniforms in around 1946. Led by Chief Petty Officer Stoko.

...ily, and used to stop and watch these Italian ...soners of war. They seemed quite happy to ...t to little girls. I don't know how that would ... viewed now! But we were quite happy ... talk to them and they spoke quite good ...glish. I think there was an Italian prisoner ... war camp fairly close. It was probably at ...estbrook. You went under the railway line ...d I think that's where it was. The back of ...here the Pheasant Garage is now. Under that ...lway bridge and out the other side. In those ...ys, I was friendly with the farm children and ...ould remember going round the farm and ...th the tractor driver, sitting on the very wide ...eel arch! Susan and I would go and find eggs ...d it was a happy childhood. I do remember ...e of the big barns in that farm was filled up ...th tins of condensed milk, which must have ...me up from the condensery at Nestlé's and ...en stored up there and the feral cats used to ...ve kittens in amongst all this. We spent many ... happy hour playing with the kittens and ...mbing on these boxes. Huge boxes, filled to ...e brim with tins of condensed milk.

Doris Roddham

...eing the Spitfires

...ne day I was out playing and I looked up ...d I could see this plane and it had a black ...oss on it. As I did so, the siren went. Mother ...me out. 'Come on in, come on in' she said. ... I went in and looked out the window ...whether I should have done it or not, but I ...d! From our house we could look right away ...er to Chequers Hill and beyond skywise. I ...ddenly saw this Spitfire, that had come up to ...ase this plane as it was going over towards ...istol. I saw it go round and as it turned ...und into the wind, because it was going ...wards Colerne – presumably to land, it blew ... and I just couldn't believe my eyes. It just ...ew up and there was just a mass of flames. It ...opped at the Pheasant. We heard later that a

Land Girl was going to work at what is now all Sainsbury's and that, but there was a farm there. She was cycling down the drive as this Spitfire blew up and it fell in front of her and she was traumatised for a long, long time.

Shirley Ritchens

Making food go further

Of course it was some time before the rationing went off. We all thought that as soon as the war was over that rationing would end. But it was several years. You had your coupons – it was an awful job to make them go round. Occasionally there was a bit on the black market! Course we were lucky in some ways, because both my sisters married farmers. So we had help, if they came to see us they would always bring milk or a chicken or something like that … so we were better off then. I often look back and wonder however mother provided the good meals that she did. We were never short of anything.

Elizabeth Perrett

A real treat!

I remember the ration books and going shopping with my mother. We used to go into Malmesbury when we were at Sherston and then naturally we came to Chippenham. We used to open the page and have these pens and mark off a little bit, you could only have that little bit. I mean – what you get today is incredible. I know I was poorly once with measles and tonsillitis and I don't know who stayed home with me, but I know my mother went shopping and she brought me home a treat. 'It was a job to get, but I was able to get it!' and it was a banana! I always remember her saying that! One banana – and she said it was a real treat! Just couldn't get the fruit and that then, years ago, but I always remember that!

Jean Brind

Make do and mend

During the war you had coupons, you had clothing coupons. I know I always had a friend of my father's daughter's school dresses, she was ever such a big person and my mother used to alter them and make them for me. I used to hate it really, but I always had a new dress every summer. As I grew, the dresses grew! Quite a lot of that went on.

Sybil Lovelock

A banana concoction

The old Scout hut was changed into a British Restaurant and I know my mother used to help there – perhaps once a week and we used to go there for our lunches – about a shilling I think, or 1s 6d. I don't know where the food came from, because it was rationed. One th that we didn't have was bananas, I remem my mother used to make some sort of c coction out of parsnips and with a flavour bananas, it was quite a good substitute, used spread it on bread and butter.

David

Feeding the pets

The veterinarian group, they also distribu dog meat and cat meat and that was meat t had been condemned. It would have be boiled very well and it was dyed green so t people would not want to eat it. People wo line up for this meat twice a week up at veterinarian group – it was at Clift Hou opposite St Paul's church. That was an imp

A group at Lowden School celebrate the end of the war, 1945.

it source because people wanted their pets
d it was hard. You couldn't give them meat,
cause we didn't have enough for ourselves.
at was the biggest shortage.

Avice Wilson

weets on ration

do remember sweets being on ration and
used to go shopping on a Saturday morn-
g with my mother. We were each given a
ry small triangular bag with I guess about
o ounces of sweets in it. That had to really
t us all the week. I do remember Easter
she used to manage to keep the chocolate
sweet ration by long enough to buy one
ormous hollow Easter egg. It used to sit on
p of the Welsh dresser and with five of us in
e family – I've two sisters and two brothers,
younger than me – on Easter Sunday, she
tched it down and she would break a piece
f for each of us and put it back where we
uldn't reach it. Each day after that until it
as gone, we had a piece of Easter egg. I don't
ink that we really suffered at all though. We
ever went hungry. My mum, I don't know
w she managed it – but through all the war
ars we never went without a meal, never
ent hungry, even if it was dripping on toast
something.

Marian Stickland

agdolls for Christmas

We did have the sirens going off at night. We'd
down into the air-raid shelter, sometimes
e hid under the stairs in the house. And I
ink because of the war, you got to know all
f your neighbours and they became friends
d they all mucked in and did things together
d helped each other. Looking back now I
alise that the neighbours used to get together
the evenings in different houses and make
ings for the children for Christmas. My

mum along with her friends, were making rag
dolls, so we all got rag dolls for Christmas, you
know. We loved them to bits.

Margaret Smith

Bombers passing overhead

When they bombed Coventry and all the
places up north, they came across here and
presumably they came from France. In swarms,
I call them swarms! Mother used to go to the
top of the garden, because our garden was
very long, and stand there shaking her fist
at them every morning after they'd go over
… if you went into the field at the top of
us, there was all these silver pieces of paper
where they'd dropped it. So they couldn't get
onto the radar or whatever it was. Also I can
remember standing on the top and looking
across to Bath and the sky was brilliantly red,
where the fires were.

Shirley Ritchens

Joining in the celebrations

In '45 we cycled into Chippenham because
they had a big celebration thing in the Market
Place and there was dancing and balloons.
It was a lovely evening. The flags out and
bunting. It was absolutely packed! To try and
dance, it was a bit difficult because there was
so many there. But I do remember that. We
cycled there from Sherston. Mum, dad and I.
That was really nice.

Jean Brind

VE Day celebrations

I remember the flags going up for VE Day
and I can remember the general celebrations
and people cheering. And then a few weeks
later my father took me up to London. He
managed to get tickets to go to London to see
his mother, who had been up in London all

Coronation party held in Culverwell's field, Lowden, 1953.

through the war, and that particular weekend the war against Japan ended. I can't remember whether it was a Saturday or a Sunday when that actually happened, but I'm pretty certain it was a weekend. We were down at Richmond when we first heard the news that the Japanese had surrendered. People were happy. Speaking to one another, whereupon a few minutes ago they were passing one another by, then all of a sudden people just talked to one another. What a relief! And then the pubs filled up and when we got back to where my gran lived, then obviously they were out in the evening to the pub and the pubs filled up and obviously people had as good a time as they possibly could.

Norman Stacey

Celebrating in the streets

We had a street party in our street. All got th tables and chairs out into the middle of th road and everybody made something to add the table. We had a really good time. Buntii we made out of old clothes, stitched togethe and we had a whale of time. There was gam as well. What we actually played now I dor remember. But I know we were out the for a long, long time during the day. Not ju eating but having some fun as well. I suppo we'd have probably played tags and racin games, like races at school. Egg and spoo race and things like that. I don't remember a the details now. I wasn't very old – I was onl about five.

Marian Sticklar

six

Chippenham Life

Flags flying in the High Street in 1953 for the Coronation of Queen Elizabeth II.

The Cottage Hospital

I was born at the Chippenham and District Hospital – Chippenham Cottage Hospital as it was called – and it was unusual for children to be born there. It was normally the nursing home in Marshfield Road, but my mother had difficulties with her first baby and she lost it at birth and I was born by Caesarean section. So they had to go up the hospital, because at that time they had an operating theatre attached to the hospital. Money for the operating was entirely supplied by the Carnival, which used to be called the Hospital Carnival and they supplied a lot of equipment for the hospital and it was run by one or two of the local doctors who were able to do minor operations – as opposed to having to go to Bath or other hospitals for the operation. I lived my early childhood at Monkton Hill. The house was owned by Bulwark I think at one time, because our back windows faced on a yard which was occupied by the Bulwark Transport. It was quite handy really, because we only had to open our window and they come along – give them a jug and they'd fill it up with fresh milk straight out the tanker. The house next door – it was all one house at one time, because the next door house had an attic and they could walk over the top of our house but we couldn't get into our attic at all. We had a cellar underneath whereas they didn't, or the door was in our house for the cellar. The chappy that lived next door was the foreman of the mill at the bottom of Monkton Hill – Mr Walker. I lived there until I was about twenty-one. It's a funny little house because it had flagstone floors, and my mother and father had to go through my bedroom to get to their bedroom. It was very old.

Don Lit

...w of Chippenham looking east, from the top of the milk factory chimney.

...aying the rent

...hen we moved to Chippenham we had a little ...ttage in Monkton Hill, and it belonged to Lady ...uriel Coventry that lived in the big house. And ...I always remember that because our rent was ...n shillings a month, and my job once a month ...as to take ten shillings up to Monkton House, ...ng the front doorbell, 'Could I speak to her ...dyship?', then they'd take me in and she'd say ...Morning Beazer'. I said 'Morning m'lady' – I had ...I doff my cap, hand over ten shillings and, well, ...e was a Lady, she was Lady Muriel. But she was ...charge of the Means Test. You probably know ...hat the Means Test is, and she used to go all ...und the houses of people like me that were in, ...e in our circumstances and say, 'Well, you don't ...ed that table, you can sell that, you can get some ...oney for that one'. She was like that and she used ...wear a tweed suit with big woollen stockings.

Norman Beazer

Living in Emery Lane

We had a very small cottage in Emery Lane, surrounded by a huge garden. We had apple trees, plum trees, a pear tree, a greengage tree, gooseberries, raspberries, red currants, white currants, black currants – you name it we had it all! And my father was quite keen on gardening, he grew all the vegetables for us. But it was a very small cottage and you walked up the garden path and walked into what we used to call the passage. I can remember it had an old table in with an aspidistra on the table. Everybody had those in those days! On the left-hand side was the wash house as we called it. With the boiler in and we didn't have a sink until quite later on. We just had a bench with the wash basin and what-not on and we had an outside loo like everyone else did and then there was the living room, which had the big old black lead grate that mother used to cook on. Then we went straight into the pantry and up to the top of the stairs and you went into the bedroom, which my grandmother slept in and I had to sleep with my mum and dad in their bedroom on the side, which was a big bedroom. I had a very, very happy childhood. In the beginning we had a paraffin lamp, a big one and it gave out a good light and my mother used to clean it and clean the wicks or granny did and we had candles to go to bed with. Of course going to the outside loo – you had the candle with your hands round it! In the winter to wash upstairs in the wash basin was jolly cold. We had the old tin bath round the fire once a week, it was lovely. In fact when I got a house with a bathroom in, I didn't like it! It was too cold! So I had a very happy childhood. We might have been poor but we didn't go without anything.

Margaret Smith

Love's the butchers

The best thing I used to do when I was a boy – Saturday mornings, I used to take one shilling and two pence, down to Love's the butchers at the bottom of Station Hill, and get a shilling's worth of beef and two penny worth of fat to go on the top and my mother would cook that for Sunday, cold for Monday, min for Tuesday and something else Wednesday something like that and when it come towa the weekend we had the bread and drippi what she made with the fat. Wonderful w my mother could do.

Brian Tins

Keeping a smallholding

My father worked at Westinghouse as a too maker and he had a sort of smallholding well as the cottage at Kellaways. Well we h about four acres of land. An acre of gard – he was a very keen gardener, he used show in the local flower show. He got go prizes for his vegetables. He bred pigs a chickens and at one time we even had sor heifers. He used to go around Chippenha and the villages delivering his produce a things that he'd grown. You see we had t acre of garden where the house was and the opposite side of the road we had t smallholding with a garage, which I think w originally a barn. Converted it to a garage a then there was stables. Only a little stable a the place where he used to breed pigs. I was a great pig breeder, only in a small w mind you and pigsties and such like. Not th

Above left: Audrey Barter (*née* Thomas) among the pigs and chickens at Kellaways, 1923.
Above right: Members of the Thomas family outside their home near Kellaways, Langley Burrell, in the early 1930s.

Major Brinkworth rowing on the canal wharf in 1895. Major Brinkworth had a coal business at the wharf.

they were nearly like the sty you would have in this day and age. We kept chickens and at one time we had four heifers that he brought in until they were ready to kill, I suppose. In the mornings the hens would all have mash, which was made from potato peelings which were boiled up and mixed with bran or oat-meal or something and sharp sand.

Audrey Barter

The old brickworks

There was a cinder path at the end of the shops in Lowden and this track led straight through to the brickworks. I can just remember seeing the old kilns there and the chimneys, I can't really remember people working there, but I think they must have been. I'm not sure when that brickyard closed. Stretched right over there, right the way from the back of the Co-op shop, it stretched right the way over to the back to Rudmans ... went right through to that area. And there were some very deep ponds there, I remember they were dangerous and I seem to recollect somebody was drowned there when I was a youngster.

Alan Horner

Lighting the lamps

The gasman come round. I can remember him cycling round Parkfields with his long pole, turning the lights on. Yes it was all gas. Well in fact we had gas lights in Parkfields until we went down to Battle Abbey. I can remember while we were down there the electric people put a lighting point in each room and a couple of plug points for free, if you said you'd have electric and I know when we came back, we had electric which was something different.

John Lovelock

The old Town Mill pictured in 1956.

The old canal

I used to go fishing up the old canal up Seend way in me younger days. I still remember the old horse-drawn barges coming along – the odd one you'd have to haul your line in for, to let them pass, you know. Mother told me the barges used to come down in the water field, by the bus station, back in her day. I didn't realise the canal ran along Pewsham there and yet I've been up most fields on farm machinery, mowers mostly. Following around because in those days the farmers couldn't bring 'em into the workshop it was too slow a job, you know, hauling them in with the war, so you had to go out there and repair 'em. I didn't know the canal was just a couple of fields over.

John Goodway

The Town Mill

As a youngster I used to have a small trike. I used to run down the road to the corner of Monkton Hill. The old mill was still there in those days and I was fascinated when these horse-drawn carts and lorries used to come along the side of the mill. And the rope used to come down from a trap door up at the top and used to hoist the grain or whatever it was. I was fascinated to see it disappear through the roof. There must have been a flood that winter, because I can remember people crossing the Town Bridge on lorries, predominantly Nestlé's lorries. The two parts of the town were cut off.

Frank White

Living by the mill

On the Monkton Hill side of the mill, right up, nearly to the roof, there was a little platform with a pair of doors on that used to open inwards. And the lorries used to pull up on Monkton Hill with the sacks of grain and they'd put a rope round the top and they used

he demolition of Spinks' stationary shop on the Bridge in the early 1960s.

pull up to this little building. As they pulled up, the floor would open, and the grain would go up and drop down onto the floor and then they loaded the grain into where hey ground it inside. Of course, that was a ovely mill and there was about eight grinding tones in there all along.

Norman Beazer

Dismantling the bridge

was working in the dairy when they hanged the bridge over the river in the own. Wonderful setting there with those bal- strade things they had. All the way along the ide there. It was wonderful, the only thing vas the river used to flood. I can remember nyself being at school and the water used to ome up as far as the Black Horse, where the 3lack Horse is now — from Woolworths. And early every year the wooden bridge where Avonside is, down the bottom of Gladstone

Road — down there — there was a wooden footbridge over the river and nearly every winter when the flood did come up it got washed away and they had to put a new one up! There was a pub down there called the Lamb I think it was. Wonderful place.

Brian Tinson

Delivery by horse and cart

From what I can remember of the railway, we used to get quite a bit come by rail, you know. Machinery spares from London and that and they used to be delivered with a horse and wagon. Bonnie Freegard he was, he had this old shire horse and his clapped-out wagon and he used to come and deliver stuff all round the town with that horse, and when he took it in his head to go, he'd go and no holding him! Course there was not traffic about them days and he used to tear up the High Street, flat out, if he took a fit in his head. Used to put

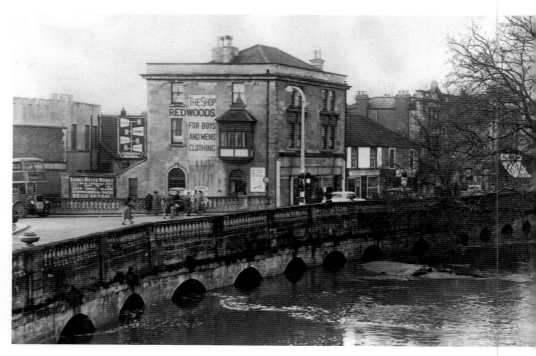

View of the Town Bridge in 1960 showing the long range of arches and branches of the old plane tree.

the fear of Christ in me. See him going, but I never knowed him have an accident and that. A strong old horse, there's no holding him, but he used to come to our place. Also he'd go down the Oxo. One day he had two big West of England sacks on there to go down the Oxo. That was parsnip seed in them and those sacks were big because they'd hold hundredweight of corn, you can tell how many parsnip seeds you'd get in a sack that size. They used to be ground up to go in the Oxos. But he had a habit of dropping bits off the wagon till one day, he had a box of spice, I think it was, for Square Deal Café round there, and it must have fell off the wagon somewhere on his rounds. He knew he had it to deliver, but when he went round there later on just to see ... somebody had picked it up, took it in the Square Deal and had a meal on the strength of it!

John Goodway

The old cemetery

Down on the opposite side of Wood Lane was the small cemetery, which was closed up long before my time. I still know a lady whose grandmother was the last lady to be buried in there and sadly, when it was going to be altered poor gran is a little bit out on the pavement somewhere! But it had a lovely little chapel, and a little walk through. Beautiful graves and of course it had these glass domes with wax flowers in from the Victorian times, presumably. We kids used to get in there, we were a bit older then, we used to get in there. Never done any damage though, because we realised that was sacred. We used to play cards in the chapel!

Peggy Burgess

Hearing the hooters

The Bridge Centre wasn't there. It was a working Nestlé's milk factory and I can

Ronnie Freegard pictured with Champion at the Chippenham Horse Show, Monkton Park, *c.* 1946.

remember the noise of the milk churns which were brought into the factory. The clanking of them and the lorries taking them away. And I can remember the steam was got up with the steam trains and they let the steam off at six o'clock in the morning. Now which factory was it that had a hooter that went off? It could've been Westinghouse or it could have been Nestlé's. There were two factory chimneys weren't there – Nestlé's had one and there was one to the left, up behind Providence Terrace, somewhere there. Those two chimneys came down. I can remember cows walking up the A4 to get to the Market Place, which had moved from the Market Place outside the Angel, down towards the river, when they pulled down River Street. Sometimes cows would run away and they'd come galloping up and in through the gate of the Ivy. And of course the Oxo factory was working, down by the river. That had a chimney too. The day was sort of punctuated with the hooter going off at one o'clock, that sort of thing. Very useful if you're working in the garden. In my great-grandfather's time, he rang the bell in the bell cote at one o'clock and you had to go up to a bedroom to do it. Then the family and the gardeners and so on would know it was time to go in to lunch.

Susan Rooke

Life along the river

There was a blacksmith's up on the wharf and we used to go up and watch the blacksmith shoeing. That was quite a business, you know, horses were being shoed all the time up there. And down the bottom of River Street there was a slaughterhouse, the children used to walk down there and see everything going on. I think I can just remember the bottom there – River Street. There was one or two pubs

Staff of Wiltshire Creameries Ltd in 1924.

down the bottom there. Solway the under-taker, I think he had his premises down there.

They had a footbridge on the Monkton Hill side and then they replaced the old bridge. Opposite where Nestlé's was on the riverside there was an island there and you could only get across to it by going down by what is now Superdrug, there was a path down there and a little bridge across. There were allotments on there. People used to hire them or rent them I suppose. As kids we used to go down the back of Nestlé's, there was a good place for fishing. I think some of the waste milk products came into the river there and attracted the fish. The bottom of River Street, at one time there was what they called Back Avon Bridge, but I don't remember it. I remember the tannery, seeing all the skins hung up on racks.

David Hall

An excuse to see the floods

When we were at school, when we heard that it was flooded I always used to say I had to go out

and do some shopping for mum, but it was ju an excuse to go over the river in the horse an cart! Over the bridge right up to Smith's an all those places were flooded, before the new bridge was built. It was a lovely old bridge. Pit they didn't build a bypass round the town an leave that as it were. Lovely old mill there an the big plane trees. The swans used to nest ther most springs, at the foot of the plane tree.

Elizabeth Perre

Harsh winters

In the cold winter – was it '63 or '64, that kin of date – the river froze and people were skat ing on the river above the bridge, up by th Common Slip there. I didn't actually skate on the river there because I thought, you know running water underneath wasn't a very good idea, so I went and skated on Corsham Lake Which probably wasn't very sensible either The snows came down on 29 December. We were out at a party at Lacock Abbey and we got home alright. Fifty-nine days after the firs

ostcard view showing the wooden structure of the Back Avon Bridge, *c.* 1905.

ll of snow, we thought the roads might be
pen enough to go for a drive, just to view
1em. We got north of Avebury and there was
ill ten-foot drifts on the side of the road.
:hippenham was cut off, no roads – in or out
 were negotiable. Helicopters had to take
roceries and bread and things to the vil-
iges and the farms, the isolated places. Castle
Combe didn't have any water for three weeks,
ecause the pipes froze in the roads. The trac-
ors took bowsers of water to the village and
hey had to bucket the stuff.

The '68 flood was particularly foul, because
eople's fuel oil got into it and so on. It flowed
ver the top of the bridge. Buses couldn't
lrive through it. They'd drop their customers
t the bottom of Lowden Hill, turn round and
o back. Tractor and trailer might transport
eople from New Road to the High Street
nd back again.

I think it was the '68 flood, there were two
najor floods in twenty-four hours. One which
:ame out of the heavens and the other was the
iver coming up. The river came up to such a

degree that it was flooded right past the Ivy
front door, up the lawn. You couldn't get in or
out of the drive. Dustbins and stone urns and
the signpost for Providence Terrace came sailing in at the front gate, because the brook came
up, you see, in Foghamshire. Because the water
rushed off the road it took all the gravel out of
the drive and threw it into the field. So that all
had to be spaded up and put back again.

Susan Rooke

Four-hour tailbacks

They said it was the bridge causing the flooding and that it wasn't enough of a span for the
water to get under and then it was causing
problems way down in Bath. One time in the
sixties the tailback was about four hours for
people getting in from Calne and getting over
that bridge. So we opened up the Salvation
Army hall and we had the tea urn out on the
front there by the gates and we had loads of
these polystyrene cups making tea and hand-
ing them to the drivers of lorries and cars as

Buses get through the floods of 1963.

they were going by, because they'd been stuck for about four hours … and we had young-sters, I mean my own son and daughter were out on the bridge helping to push cars out through the water. Quite a day, quite a day… So our bridge got demolished and a new modern bridge put in its place and it hasn't improved it at all.

Margaret Smith

Floods in the '30s

It used to come over the Town Bridge and it cut Chippenham absolutely in two when it was like that. Westinghouse was on one side, Nestlé's was on the other side, the laundry was the other side – the work really was more the other side. People that lived up Wood Lane and London Road area, they used to have these lorries coming across to take the girls, but it was really quite dangerous because it got so deep. We often used to think what if

all uptips – the girls could have been thrown into the river. Once when it was up like that my dad walked all round Black Bridge t get home, but he said he'd never do it agai – from Westinghouse round Black Bridge an round by the bathing field. But it must hav been quite mucky all round there.

Peggy Chamberlai

Viewed from the bus

I remember the floods. I was at school ther and I used to have a friend who lived i Lacock and quite often I would catch the bu from school and go across to Lacock. Thi particular time, I was on a double-decker bu coming up through the town and saw all th shoes floating in the water from Freema Hardy and Willis, which was a shoe sho down there. Obviously the flood had broker their windows and being in a high bus, we were able to go up through the town. But

Flooding in the High Street, September 1927.

...an remember that quite distinctly. It went a long way, the floods, through the town at that time. But then they got the weir fixed further out and that stopped, but that was quite a memory.

Doris Roddham

Living by the river

Well, we were poor, let's put it that way and we lived in this cottage up in Monkton Hill and there was no gas or electricity. We had a paraffin oil heater with two burners in the corner, there was a coal-burning copper, where mum did her washing and all that. And she used to cook the Christmas pudding in there. That was a funny little house that was. We had an outside toilet, but it was only a bucket. There was no such thing as inside toilets. We had oil lamps. That was when the weir was there you see, and because it was right on the side of the river, when the floods came and the level of the river rose, the water used to seep through the floor of our kitchen.

Norman Beazer

The price of a rabbit

There was a big orchard by the cottage where we lived and dad'd go out there in the orchard and prop hisself up against a tree with his gun and I'd get sent out round the field and tap the hedge all the way round. Sometimes we were lucky, turn a rabbit out you know and get him coming the right way. During the war George Flower used to collect rabbit skins and bottles and rags and that. At one time rabbit skins got up to 1s 6d and I mean that was quite a lot of money in them days. I know a chap used to bring me uncle in a rabbit and he'd skin 'em there and then and give uncle the rabbit and nip in George Flower's with the rabbit skin, ... used to make hats with, trilby hats I think. I can't remember in those days, but I should

The last meeting of the Board of Guardians of the Workhouse. Mr Hodgkinson, the master, standing fifth from left, and his wife the matron seated second from the right beside Dr Ayres.

The Great Western Hotel, left, and New Road viewed from the railway embankment in the 1930s.

bove left: Charlie Gribble walking across the Town Bridge. Charlie worked as a cobbler for the Co-op from a small *ned* in Westmead in the 1930s.
bove right: Joe Buckle (right) chats to Mr Coventry on the platform at Chippenham Station in the 1940s.

hink, you know that a rabbit sold for perhaps our shillings. George Flower only had a car nd trailer just to collect it with then. He sed to get Collier to collect the scrap from Westinghouse. He always had the contract at Westinghouse. I think the war made him.

John Goodway

Seeing the workhouse

There was Mr Wilkins that had a wooden leg, ie was at the workhouse, and then there was little fella, he used to go shopping for the vorkhouse, used to push a truck and do the hopping. And then there was another little nan – he always had a big fob watch in his pocket and he had a funny little hat.

We used to go up there for a walk and see he people behind the bars, because they had people that were not quite normal and they had them in, like a round, circular place with big iron bars so that they couldn't get out. I had a very old aunt up there when I was a little girl, 'cause she was ill and no-one to look after her, so they put her up there. Girls that had babies before they were married – they had the babies up there which were left for adoption, also. They said that the tramps would put their money in this particular wall before they went into the workhouse, so that their money wouldn't get stolen. I don't know if it was true, but that's what I've heard. I think the master wore a suit. I know the matron had a hat and the navy blue and a white bib.

Margaret Smith

Local characters

There was a chap called Chevron worked for George Flower. Had a trolley and was a rag-

and-bone man. Used to go round the streets shouting 'Rags and Bones' and he was a bit of a character. He used to put the children on his trolley and do a dance, dance about in the street! Well I suppose there weren't the traffic. And there was a chap named Jimmy Davis too. He was a little bit eccentric, but he used to push a trolley too. He worked for somebody, but he always had a buttonhole and used to come to church on a Sunday night. Sit up on the front row, on the left-hand side. Amazing, some lovely characters in those days. This chap Chevron, apparently he once went to sleep in a coffin for a bet, round by the back of the Neeld Hall. People used to go round and see him asleep in this coffin! And there was a lady who lived round the Butts. And she used to walk miles round the streets of Chippenham – knitting! – and she wore black. Had a black hat, I think. She was known as Knitting Molly

and she used to walk miles continuously knitting as she walked! She was an oldish lady, should think – fifty, sixty odd.

David Ha

Queen Mary's visit

I saw Queen Mary when she came t Westinghouse. That was the old lady, Kin George V's wife. She came to Westinghous and we were all allowed to stand on th veranda to see her go round. She had he photograph taken with some of the old peopl there, you know. The oldest workers, I thin it was. There was a photograph of her at Jo Buckle's shop I'm sure, with her stood u there. And when she come that day, all th streets was all decked out, everything, yo know, it was so different.

Freda Curti

Queen Mary tours Westinghouse during her visit to Chippenham in 1942.

seven

Shops

Horse-drawn hearses stand in station yard in the early 1900s.

The Little George

I can always remember from my very young days coming into Chippenham with a horse and cart from Kington St Michael. The Little George had a hostelry and we used to put up the horse and trap there and then mother would go down the town and do her shopping. And all shops had errand boys and they used to take the stuff back up to the Little George until we were ready to go. What always fascinated me at the Little George, was the array of the horses for the funerals, the plumes and elaborate harnesses hanging on the wall. They were just hanging there, you see. It was Mr and Miss Daniels, and I think they used to supply the horses for the funerals. Because father bought a horse from them once, Darky, and when Mr Daniels had a funeral, this horse

it always had to go back – and officiate. But also they used to be very useful, because you could leave your bikes there. I think it was a penny to leave them there during the week and tuppence on Saturdays. But Saturday used to get terribly crowded, because people came into town for the pictures and from all the places around. My bike always seemed to be at the bottom of this big pile, but it was quite a trick to get your bike. If you were one of the early people who went there, your bike was right underneath everyone else's.

Elizabeth Perren

Fish and fruit

Old Mr Joyce used to come round with his horse and cart with fruit and vegetables. The

A view of the half-timbered building that housed Joe Buckle's fish shop and Doswell's confectioners, in the Market Place in the 1930s.

was every Tuesday and every Saturday and course, 'cause my dad had a shop at Corsham, they always had a natter. He always used to say 'Yes, what would you like?', but we always had an apple. Never mind what we liked, we always had an apple. We used to go to Stents for the fish. Down the bottom of Station Hill, that's where dad used to get his fish and fruit from. He used to bring me over in the holidays. He had a motorbike and sort of a sidecar made so that he put his fish and fruit in it. Joe Buckle, he had a fish shop and he's another friend of my dad's, 'cause my dad used to get fish there as well, you see. And our mum would give me a shilling and say to me, 'Oh, go along Joe Buckle's and get a couple of kippers' or something like that, you know.

Freda Curtis

Joe Buckle's shop

I mean amazingly there was Joe Buckle's fish shop for instance. It was a half-timbered building and the front of the shop was open to the street totally. You didn't go into the shop, it was open, you walked straight in. In his early time of course it was festooned with pheasants and turkeys and geese and such at Christmas.

Susan Rooke

Mr Gee's joint!

My father was a great one for the Co-operative. The Co-operative society! The Co-op in Chippenham was quite a large establishment. It stretched where Wilkinson's is now and my father used to go in there and he used to embarrass me. During the war things were in short supply. Oranges'd appear, everybody would come out of the woodwork saying oranges or bananas available at so-and-so. He used to go in there and he knew all the staff there very, very well including the manager, because I believe in those days it was all very democratic and you had a committee that ran it and he was quite a leading light within the committee. So he would go in there and say 'Right, what have you got?' Ex-serviceman, four children and he used to make me cringe! He used to use his north country accent, which I found appalling. 'Ere, ere lad. I've got four kids and an ex-serviceman, you know – what have you got going cheap?' I used to feel so big! And I knew a lot of them by name within the Co-op. In the Co-op in those days they used to have a system. You'd have a little notebook and you wrote down all the goods you wanted and they'd make up an order and they would deliver it. Well I suppose later in the war that ceased and so on a Friday, when I was at Ivy Lane, I would be given the great honour of going round and collecting 'the joint' – and that doesn't mean something you smoked! – it meant a hunk of meat on a bone! I'd go and say 'Have you got Mrs Gee's joint?' and they'd produce this piece of meat!

Michael Gee

The Miss Honniballs

The railway arch was Honniball's warehouse. The Miss Honniballs. You could never forget it! There was two sisters who wore black skirts down to their ankles, and white frilly fronted blouses, as they would have worn before the First World War – I think! Their hair was done up in a bun and huge diamond earrings, I mean really big ones! They didn't believe in display at all. There were just rough wooden shelving really and you walked round sort of sideways and there'd be crazy heaps of plates and saucers and cups all piled up. Any old

pattern, you know. You had to look for wha you wanted. She had a tremendous store i her warehouse of coloured china and sh would bring out odd things all through th war, because you couldn't get coloured chin patterned china – it was all white in the wa If you went in there carefully, time and tim again you could build up a tea service o whatever it was you wanted! They had a lad working for them who we nicknamed 'th slave' who had to work like mad! And a ma – Cornish, and he had to do allsorts … an they had a greengrocer's shop next door. S it was the two shops – the porcelain and th greengrocer's shop. If you bought anything i the greengrocer's shop – which one did ever now and again, you had to run the gauntl of buying overripe fruit, because it hadn't sol and she wanted to get rid of it. I remembe buying grapes there once, and I said 'I don want the yellow ones I want the green one – 'Oh they're all yellow!' same as she used t say 'All the china is chipped', and she'd do th – chip, chip, chip! I mean it was wonderfu They lived over the shop. When the river use to come up, the shop and everything woul get flooded. Well I suppose if they thought th flood was coming in the shop, they'd put th greengroceries up as high as they could. Chin wouldn't matter getting muddy, so they'd leav it there and wash it afterwards!

Susan Rook

China, fruit and a tabby cat

The shops in Chippenham were so differen in those days. All old-fashioned shops. Mis Honniball's on the Bridge with the big chin shop. Masses and masses of china on each sid of the long shop and up the middle. Mothe used to take me in there absolutely terrifie that I was going to knock something down. had to hold on to her tight all the time! Th Honniballs were sisters and they had a littl

ery early picture of Honniball's shop on the corner of the Bridge and Foghamshire.

it shop next door – a greengrocer's, where
Avon weir was. They wouldn't be allowed
have it now, because they had the fruit and
vegetables – they were always in decay in
winter and the cat was always asleep in the
ddle of them! A lovely tabby cat right in the
ddle of all this. Like made itself a nest!

Elizabeth Perrett

Couch the chemist

ere was Mr Couch the chemist. Mr Couch
s the place everybody used to go if they
nted anything. Whatever problems you had,
u'd go and see Mr Couch instead of going
the doctor. We went to Dr Hickson, who
d his practice up Lowden Hill. I thought it

was lovely, because it had a lovely garden and
it went right down to the Bath Road. I think
there's about three houses now, on where his
garden was. At the back a whole group of
houses. I used to think that was nice.

Sybil Lovelock

To be an errand boy

Another thing I wished to do was to be an
errand boy. There was a little shop around the
corner, I don't know whether it still exists, in
Greenway Lane. It's called Failey's and it was a
local grocery shop. They used to do deliveries
on bikes and they had these bikes which had
two legs came down and you hoiked it back so
that it lifted the bike up. But there was a huge

PLEASE USE THIS BLOTTER.

THE KING OF TONICS.

For Great Weakness! Loss of Appetite!
Depression of Spirits! Loss of Energy!

TAKE

COUCH'S TRI-TON
(The Three Tonics)

For the BRAIN, BLOOD and STOMACH.

COUCH'S TRI-TON

Takes away "THAT BORN-TIRED FEELING."

Sold in large Bottles, 1/- each.

PREPARED ONLY BY

W. COUCH, Chemist and Druggist,
By Examination.

MARKET PLACE, CHIPPENHAM.

Above: Advertising blotter produced by Mr Couch, chemist.

Left: Mr W. Couch the chemist, outside his shop in the Market Place

hael Gee enjoys a ride on a friend's motorbike.

ket on the front … I would have loved to
ve got my hands on one of these machines.
d again that was 'No, you know that is not
the likes of you'.

Michael Gee

etting the milk

hink everyone must have had milk in those
s because the milkman used to come round
 back and just plonk the milk outside the
k door. Bottles then. Up to the war, it must
ve been in churns, it was in churns when
 moved into Beechwood Road. In the days
Kington St Michael, we had to fetch the
lk from a farm. My mother used to employ
ittle schoolgirl to go up to the farm and
 the milk for us. We used to send a little
lk can up and they used to measure it out.
emember when you got the milk in the

morning it would still be warm – the cream
used to rise to the top.

My brother-in-law started a milk round in
Jacksoms Lane when he was alive. He had old
churns to take round and he'd measure the
milk when he got round there. That was in
the 1940s.

Elizabeth Perrett

Around the Co-op

There used to be the Co-op shop at the top
and I think that was built in about 1922. I think
there's a stone on there somewhere, and that
was quite a lively place. You had the big general
shop there and I recollect the old-fashioned
hanging-the-money-on-a-wire thing and it
used to shoot around the shop to the cashier
and then come back. And then you had a nice
butcher's shop, which also was the Co-op. And

Mr John Spencer delivering for the Co-op.

then next to that butcher's shop, in the war years, was a dugout with all sandbags which was supposed to be for the Home Guard or defence thing for that area. Going back along past the Co-op there was another couple of shops there which are now a fish and chip shop, but in my time they were always empty.

Alan Horner

Getting the divvy

Divvy day was quite a thing, wasn't it? People used to queue up to go into the Co-op to get their divvy and they used to give it out in the Co-op Hall and you had old Billy Snow giving out the money. People used to really want their divvy, want their money, because if they had a big family I think it went to 1s 6d during the war. I think that was about the most they ever paid out. If I remember rightly it was about 1s 6d. I think it was about six-pence before that, was it? Sixpence on every pound. I'm sure it was sixpence, perhaps it was threepence before, in the very early times. But I know in the war it went up to about 1s 6d.

There was a Mr Jones from Derry Hill, had a greengrocery cart, he used to come on Saturday, and there was a Mr Clifford and M Hancock – the coal merchants. Mr King th oil people – where Revolutions is now – the was King's the ironmongers in Foghamshi and Mr Tucker used to come round with th oil cart on a Saturday and deliver all the para fin to people, because most of the people h paraffin lamps, you see, before the war this … and Mr Dauncey the milkman he us to come along in St Mary Street. We had lady living in St Mary Street, called Caroli Archard – in the big old house that was ne to the Congregational church. It's not the now, but you can see the outline on the ne cottage of the roof – because it was a point roof. And she had a bucket in her passagew with a shovel and if the horses did anythi we got the bucket and picked the manu up, because she used to use it on her garde Then there was a Mr Freegard, with the b old horse out our way, big horse that was – shire horse – the horse's name was Champic I think, yes. Lovely horse with the white feat

, you know. The Co-op had a horse and
rt. Mr Archard had the bread cart.

Margaret Smith

the personal touch

preferred Chippenham as it was, you know.
e used to come in. A nice way of shops
up through the town. Shopkeepers were
ways much more friendly than they are
wadays, I think. Tended to own their own
sinesses and also more of a personal touch.
ney just served you. You went to the counter
d they got you what you wanted. The gro-
rs of course, they used to weigh up the sugar
d everything. Sugar, biscuits and everything
d to be weighed up. You could buy many
ngs like that. If you had a large family those
oken biscuits must have been a great help,
cause there wasn't the money about. Bigger
nilies and not much money about.

Elizabeth Perrett

selection of shops

nippenham was very different. You had
uch better shops. You had Wheelers, fabrics
d clothes and everything you could think
There was about three shops in a row and
ere wasn't anything that Wheelers couldn't
l you! I mean – haberdashery, fabrics, every-
ing you could think of. You wouldn't go in
heeler's and ask for anything and not be
le to buy it. Then up in the Market Place
u had Stafford James. Again it was fabrics
d haberdashery and clothes. It was so many
ings. That was probably curtains and covers
d sheet and things and that, but it didn't
atter what you wanted, in Chippenham
en, you could get everything you wanted.
u had Hetherington's – a lovely man's shop,
u don't have a decent man's shop now. I
ink we've always had Boots, but we did have
Neel's the chemist – lovely old gentleman.

Just up the road a little way from Boots, Neel's
the chemist was a smashing place to go in. You
couldn't go in and not find what you wanted.
He was lovely – Mr Neel. I think he made his
own pills. On the opposite corner to Burton's
– there used to be Buckle's, the fishmongers
and it used to have a lovely marbled slab out,
with all the wet fish on it for you to buy. Don't
think we ever used to buy that much fish. But
you used to probably stop and talk when you
went by, because it was such a fascinating shop
to see all these different fish, laid out on the
marble slab and you wouldn't be able to do it
these days would you?

Marian Stickland

The old post office

Farrell's I think was up next to Woolworths,
International were up there, Newman's were
there – they started years and years before I
was born, I know. There was two or three saddlers up there just past there, you know. I suppose obviously with the horses around then,
there was a trade then for leather work and
saddlers. The post office, the old post office
was there where the building societies are
now. The boys used to come round the back
of where we worked – the telegram boys. To
start off with they were on push bikes, then
they had Bantams, later on.

John Lovelock

Memories of market day

At first the market used to be up by the Market
Place, up where the War Memorial stands.
Then they moved down to where Littlewoods
is and that market down there, and then they
moved up to the top of Station Hill. I know
when they were down by Littlewoods, there
used to be all kinds of rabbits and allsorts,
poultry of all kinds … eggs and everything
like that. It was really a general market in those

The Friday Cattle Market, pictured in the Market Place in 1906, before its removal to Borough Parade in 1907.

days. It was a great day – Chippenham was crowded with the farmers' wives. Men in the markets and the women in the shops!

Elizabeth Perrett

The cattle market

I can remember market days when they used to have the cattle up in the Market Place. Out where the Cenotaph is now. They used to have foals, foal pens round where the bus station is now, called the Wharf, round there. After that – they used to be down where Borough Parade is now. That was the Market Place in there, the cattle market. On the right-hand side as you go into Borough Parade, from the town side, I think there's still some rings in the wall, where they used to bring the bulls. Tie them up by their rings and put them in there. Not many cattle were coming in by train. A lot of them used to walk, but when I was on the railway, you used to have them going

away by train. I think the bloke's name w Lissenmore. He used to come to Chippenha market, buy cattle, bring them up the stati and send them to Chester, or somewhe like that, to sell them and get more mon for them than what he'd pay for them Chippenham. He'd send them off to Ches for next day's market. I can remember th because I used to go down there sometin when I was a little lad.

Brian Tins

To buy a tortoise

I remember when the market was up at t back of the Rose and Crown, when I wa little girl. My mother always promised me tortoise and we'd gone up to get this torto and a thunderstorm had broken out and had to shelter under some trees oppos what's the hospital now. It was the workhou in those days. By the time the thunder stor

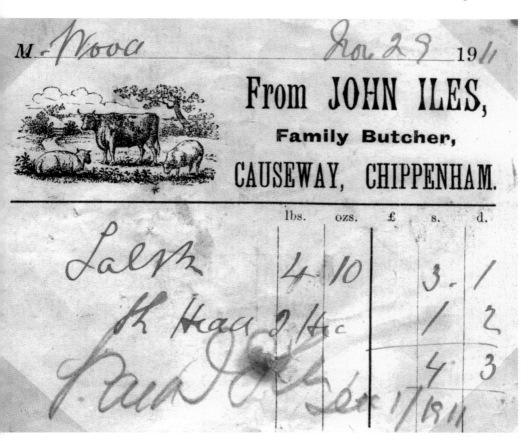

M. Wood   Nov. 29 19 11

From JOHN ILES,
Family Butcher,
CAUSEWAY, CHIPPENHAM.

	lbs.	ozs.	£	s.	d.
Calve	4	10	3	-	1
Sh Head & Fac	2	14		1	2
				4	3

Receipt from John Iles, butcher in the Causeway, 1911.

d gone over, it was too late to go and get
y tortoise, 'cause they sold all chickens and
ppies and kittens and all that sort of thing
this market, at the top there. Of course it
as probably a summer holiday or something
cause she wouldn't have taken me away
om school and it would have been a Friday,
I never did get my tortoise. I remember the
rible disappointment of it all!

Doris Roddham

oving the cattle

those days, obviously if a man was running
s own business – a family business – you
ent into say Newman's the saddlers, well

there was Mr Newman behind the store and
it was his shop. The same way as you went
into a butcher's shop, the butcher was there
– it was his shop and you were probably
aware of their personalities. A thing that was
always very interesting was the markets. I can
remember the Cattle Market being where
Borough Parade is now. So the cattle were
there and when they were sold they were
driven through the town, up Station Hill, up
to the pens in Cocklebury to go to the trains,
loaded onto the destination wherever they had
to go. On Friday afternoon the cattle would
be going through town, and obviously you
drive a few hundred cows through the town,
well there's muck everywhere! And it was

View of the Causeway showing the Five Alls Inn in 1908.

quite exciting really, 'cause you just had to get out of the way of the cattle. The shopkeepers had to close their door because they had the cattle in the shops. That was quite something on a Friday – the market and also the cattle, because the cattle were right there. There was no getting away from it and then they'd lead the bulls through as well. That was quite something that was. Pity we ever lost that, 'cause all they've done is make way for the motor car, instead of having the muck of the cows.

Norman Stacey

Shops in Sheldon

Going back to the shops, when you went on down the Sheldon Road, before you get to Lowden School, on the right-hand side was

Chappel's fruit and vegetable place. They we market gardeners and had a shop and the used to be a little old-fashioned shoe sh and the man actually used to mend shoes, h repair them. And then the wine and spir place. Interestingly, in Sheldon Road, a lit brook ran across under there and there us to be an old shop and it was run by a lady Mrs Woods. I used to think it was funny th this shop was over the brook with the wat running underneath the shop. And that was little old fruit and veg shop. And then you ha the school and across the road there used be a dairy there ... Cary's Dairy, I think ther a housing site there now. The other shop the opposite side to where Cary's Dairy w the opposite side to Park Street, I thoug there was a baker's shop there. So there w

...nes Motor Works in New Road, dressed for the carnival, *c.* 1955.

...ot of shops and then, of course, round ...wden you had more shops. There used to ...a baker's shop, a bakery, a post office, you ...lly didn't need to come into the town in ...ose days.

Alan Horner

...ops on the Bridge

...a the Bridge there were two shops. There ...s a jeweller's and there was Holland's, the ...er shop. They were on the corner of the ...dge. There was a big brass lamp in the ...ddle, then there was the bridge. The other ...e of the Bridge was Pond's, which was a pub, ...en there was the hotel, that's where Smith's ...ow, there was a hotel – the George.

Freda Curtis

Cavacutti

Cavacutti had their first shop in the Causeway. They used to sell penny lollies. I think they were the first penny lollies in Chippenham, but you had to eat them quick, because there was no preservatives or anything in them and they dripped away, just little round ones, not a lot bigger than your thumb, quite honestly. They slowly moved down the Causeway. I'm not sure when that would have been, but I've got a feeling they were probably there the whole of my childhood. Probably till I was about ten or twelve years old. Then they moved down to where the gents' hairdresser is. Then they moved down to where John had his fish and chip shop in the corner of the Market Place, near where Cole's stores used to be. And then of course they moved over

Aerial view of the town from the top of St Paul's church in 1980.

to the Waverley. I'm not sure when they came here, but he was a lovely old man. Apparently, with his family, he ruled. Still, but he brought his boys up well and their oldest is still around the town now. I went to school with one of them. I knew all the others. They were a lovely family. If you couldn't afford a lolly or something, they'd find a lump of something in the fridge for you which was quite nice! A lot of us never could afford them, whether it was deliberate or not is another matter!

Peggy Burgess

Visiting the library

I can remember going into the shops with my mother. It was quite a long way, but my mother wasn't one for going on the bus or anythi like that. Course we didn't have fridges, so t was a long trail from Rowden Road into t town two or three times a week. Used to that quite frequently. I can remember her goi into the International and having things me sured out into those little blue packets – su – and I'd sit there in the chair and she'd ord stuff and carry it off back home.

And she also enrolled me in the libra when I was little. The library isn't where it now. It was over where the Jubilee Rooms a I used to look forward to that, going into t library. My mother was a great reader. In fa more meals got burnt because she was readi than anything else! But there weren't a lot children's books, if there were I read them ve

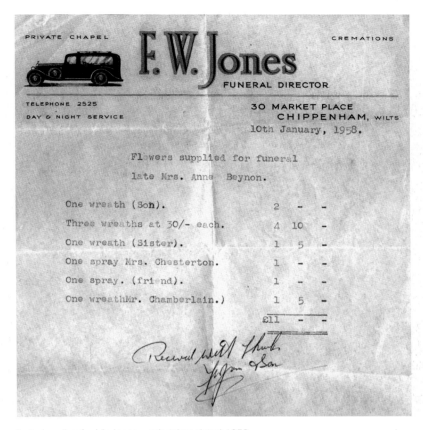

PRIVATE CHAPEL

F.W. Jones
FUNERAL DIRECTOR

CREMATIONS

TELEPHONE 2525
DAY & NIGHT SERVICE

30 MARKET PLACE
CHIPPENHAM, WILTS

10th January, 1958.

Flowers supplied for funeral
late Mrs. Anne Beynon.

One wreath (Son).	2	-	-
Three wreaths at 30/- each.	4	10	-
One wreath (Sister).	1	5	-
One spray Mrs. Chesterton.	1	-	-
One spray. (friend).	1	-	-
One wreath Mr. Chamberlain.)	1	5	-
	£11	-	-

Letterheading for Mr Jones, undertaker, dated 1958.

ickly and then I had to go onto adults and
pe that I would be interested. And I was, I
d a lot of adult books.

Doris Roddham

he sweet factory

n the corner of Dallas Road and Marshfield
oad, where there was Mr Campbell and
ell's music shop, next to that there was a
eet shop and that was a real old one – chap
med Burton and his wife or sister ran it.
hey made their own sweets. Up in St Mary's
ace – the top of St Mary's Place beyond
e Catholic church – he had a little factory
ere where they made these sweets and he
d a chap who worked for him. Put them on

a trolley, bring them down and deliver them
to the shop there. Before the war and after. I
think we must have had coupons or rations
for sweets. It was amazing that rationing went
on so long, because I was married in '53 and
when you think that just before that there was
rationing and restrictions. We accepted it and
didn't realise how serious it was.

David Hall

Billy Pearce's peppermints

My mother was the daughter of a naval
pensioner, who had a sweet shop and a
newsagent's shop in St Mary Street and he
used to make lots and lots of sweets, but
mainly peppermints. And his peppermints

went all over the world – Canada and places – and he was always known as Billy Pearce – for his peppermints! And he had a little stall in the market – I believe – on a Friday. My earliest recollection is my mother taking me to see my father's mother in Downing Street. Apparently when I got to her house I always asked for a sugar lump. She always gave me a sugar lump, and I can remember her going to the cupboard and getting the tin out with the sugar lumps in and giving me a sugar lump. That's my earliest memory, you know, the tin coming out of the cupboard.

Margaret Smith

Woolworths

Woolworths – that was still there, but a mu smaller shop and it did go back, quite narr and at the back where they've now got yo lampshades and blinds and things at the ba of it – it used to be a garden centre. You us to go up some steps and into a garden cent right at the back, and that was lovely. Th all gone with the houses and everything e that's been built there since. When I was a lit girl, the bridge was a narrow bridge, not ve much room under the spans for the water go under, and built on the top of the Brid were two shops. A newsagent's shop and jeweller's shop on the top of the Bridge. The used to be the Salvation Army hall and the were traffic lights there.

Marian Stickla

View of Lowden church and almshouses, 1900s.

eight

Sport and Leisure

Boys of the Secondary School set off for a cross-country run, pictured with Mr Tuck the headmaster on the right, in the 1930s.

Grass track cycling

In those days lots of towns and even villages used to have sports days. They'd have running events, cycling events, tug of war. I used to concentrate my cycling on the track racing. Most of it was on grass tracks. They used to have some good places – Gloucestershire, cricket ground in Bristol, Cheltenham and Devizes, and you used to get big crowds at these meetings. The highlight of the sports was always the five mile cycle race. I don't know whether people used to go there just to watch the racing or hope there'd be a crash! Which was always quite spectacular! I picked up quite a lot of prizes. Some of them came in quite handy when I was married, we had canteens of cutlery, fish knives, knives and forks, fruit spoons, oh – I had quite a collection of clocks and barometers! My cycling days came to an end a few years after I was married. Didn't have any spare cash for cycling!

Frank White

The cycling club

In Foghamshire, opposite the Consti Cl that used to be the YMCA and in the grou floor was the headquarters of the Chippenh Wheelers, and the Chippenham Red Trian Bicycle ... or something like that ... of cou that was the badge of the YMCA, a red t angle and we had quite a nice little cycli shop there. There was Bill Page and Jack Nu and Jim Carvey. One of the other chaps v a schoolmaster from Calne. Every Sunday used to meet outside and go for a little r round somewhere. If we went Bath way, always used to finish up at Jack Allen's. I do know the names of the roads, but where y go out of Bath and go under the viaduct to the Wells Road, there used to be a sort café, not a posh place, we used to always go there – Jack Allen's it was called – for tea and sandwich. I suppose, it would be about ten twelve, you know, different chaps and girls.

Norman Bea

Chippenham Ladies Croquet Club in 1921.

e Wessex Centre

her bought me a bike when I was sixteen. vas an old two stroke, funny little bike. But vas quite happy. Had an engine in it, that's I worried about. I have been a keen motorlist ever since. Our son was born 1948, it viously rubbed off on him – he was quite n on it and we both rode in motorcycle nts together.

Motorcycle trials – the group was called Wessex Centre. It's a number of clubs ether. Goes down as far as Frome, Shepton llet, Swindon, Bristol – two or three clubs Bristol. We'd all ride in one another's nts. Every September all the clubs would together and you'd all put the dates in t you want for your different events. But were on the motorcycle scrambles, grass cks. Used to run a grass track for the caral and give all the proceeds from it. Paul ynolds, just up the road, he used to let us e a field for nothing and we used to have

the scrambles up at West Yatton. The farmer out there, used to let us have his fields. I'm still in the club now – in fact a life member of it, we still run trials and I go out and help observing, marking.

John Lovelock

Field judging

In my time I've had quite a few interests. They had a Westinghouse and Chippenham Athletic Club in those days. We used to have friendly matches with Swindon, Trowbridge, Bath, Fry's, Bristol AC and all those type of local clubs. We used to have an evening match with them and I took an interest in this athletics – in the official side of it and I took an exam to be a field judge and I finally got to grade two. There is gradings in this field judge – you start off at grade four, then grade three, grade two, grade one and then chiefs and allsorts of things. I got to grade two in field judging, I took up timekeeping as well and I got to grade three in timekeeping. I used to do it for local clubs like Bristol AC, Southampton, Aldershot – because a lot of the local clubs didn't have too many big fixtures, so we used to have to travel quite a bit. I done that for quite a few years But we used to do miles in a weekend and not get a penny for it. The only time you got paid for it was if you went to one of the international matches or one of the ones in London. You'd get your expenses to go, but we used to go just for the love of it.

Don Little

Keen on cricket

When I was younger, Michael Hathaway's father, who had the factory on the old Hathaway site, he was a keen cricketer and he used to coach boys. He got a team up of local boys from the school – Ivy Lane and that. About twelve or thirteen that sort of age. We used to go up for coaching once or twice a week. Used to have games in the summer holidays.

We went up the river to the Sea Cadets area – that was the swimming pool, or it wasn't – it was a portion in the river! They had a portion I think it must have had a cement base, because it had a proper bottom over a small area where we learnt to swim. Had a high diving board. That was a character – used to go there. Mr Mortimore senior, who owned the coal factory which is the bottom of the railway steps. Now a weighbridge, but he had a coal business and the old chap lived in Marshfield Road, further up – past the hotel now. He used to go swimming every Sunday morning, always on a Sunday, and he must have been in his eighties. Used to put a towel round his neck and shuffle off down Marshfield Road, down to the High Street, all the way back to the swimming pool, and

he did that regularly all his life. They say used to break the ice in the winter and go They used to have races Christmas morn down there, but he was a character – Frog Mortimore they called him!

David

Swimming in the river

I learnt to swim out at Kellaways, which not far really from Greenway Lane, where lived, and we used to walk out to Kellaw and jump in the river there. My mother forl me to do it and I used to say I hadn't be there, but she could smell me, because y always smelled of the river when you got o We did use the river a lot. The 'bathing pla was in operation and I did go to the 'bathi place' where the Sea Cadet place is now Long Close.

Alan Hor

The old duck pond

I learnt to swim at the old duck pond, as called it up the river – where the Sea Cad are now. The old duck pond – I went there. Taught myself to swim, nowadays th wouldn't allow anyone to do it. All the wa coming straight down from the fields whe the cattle had been. Any amount of little fisl there and they used to tickle your legs wh you were in the water. I used the outdoor pc until the Olympiad opened. I was down the on the last day it was open. Never thought th by the next year it would've closed. Love pool. It was so nice, people could go in the with their children and spend all day the The trees and that lovely situation, with t hill going up there. Really a beautiful pool know people used to come from miles arou to go there.

Elizabeth Per

all-male group at Chippenham Swimming Club pose with trophies in front of the clubhouse.

hippenham Secondary School swimming gala at the bathing place on the River Avon.

Learning to swim

We used to spend so much time down there at the river in the summer, by the Sea Cadets. It was really lovely. We learnt to swim down there. We used to go from Westmead, 'cause Westmead always had a very good reputation for swimmers and there was a lady from Swindon used to come to teach us. And she would put a belt round you – put you out into the deeper part and then drag you in and that was how you learnt to swim! There was what they called the duck pond, which was a shallower piece and it had a board all the way round. So we were contained like within this board. But she did teach us to swim eventually and there was what we called the springboard, which you ran along and you could jump into the river.

The Chippenham Swimming Club ran the 'bathing place'. You used to pay 1s 6d for the summer to join the swimming club and the you could go anywhen, you know, when yo wanted to. I think you had a girls' night an a boys' night, don't think it was always mixe bathing. There was two huts that we used change in, because we went with the scho … it was freezing cold until they built tl concrete building, which is still there. Yo could sunbathe on the top there.

I remember swimming for the scho against the other schools. When I was at tl Secondary School and you had a bar, ju underneath the springboard, you used swim up to there. It was supposed to be fif yards. We had to get our certificates didn't w – twenty-five, fifty and a mile then. Up an down the river. And it was usually freezir cold weather when we had to do that. An you were in the deep all the time too.

The construction of the diving boards at the outdoor pool at Monkton Park in 1960.

The river must have been quite deep, cause they played polo there and they had ese great high diving boards there. I always member my brother played polo for the hippenham team. There was a first and a cond team and he never used to get in the st team. He was always in the second team. ney were quite – what they called dirty ayers – because the water was so murky, so ep, they used to dive underneath against eir opponent, grab hold of their legs and ill them under! And sometimes the referee dn't always see.

Peggy Chamberlain

hippenham Sailing Club

ell the Sailing Club was formed in 1959, hen the weir was being altered and the River Board wanted to get a bigger depth. Right by the Sea Cadets was the old bathing pool. The Sea Cadets had just gone into there, I think and they dug a cutting through from the bend, just downstream, and Bill Wade and a few others from Westinghouse saw it and thought that it will make an ideal sailing place. So they asked the young managers of Westinghouse if they could do this and they said 'Yes', it all formed part of their social club. So Chippenham Sailing Club was launched. We had no compounds, they just used to drive down to the bank and launch their boats. Sea Cadets helped a lot and I think at one time, when it first started, they used to launch from a garden in St Mary Street. But gradually the club started to expand and they took on people – not from Westinghouse, but from outside – that was when my husband joined

ne Sailing Club regatta on the River Avon in 1959, before the compound was developed.

Chippenham Sea Cadet Corps at their headquarters on Cocklebury Road, around 1946 or '47.

in '62. Gradually it got bigger and bigger and they got the compound. They had a hut. I joined in '64 when I became engaged to my husband. It was great fun, because there was the small hut and if it rained everybody tried to get in and you were pushing and shoving to try and get in there. We had one gas ring to put the kettle on to make the tea. There was so many boats, it was really competitive in those days and it was great fun as well.

Shirley Ritchens

Joining the Sea Cadets

When I was a young lad I wanted to join the Sea Cadet Corps, which I did. The Commanding Officer up there was a well known name in the town – Jack Cohu. We used to have some great fun there. Have the training on the

seamanship things in the classrooms, learn ing how to tie knots, read compasses and a the other things and also there was a certai amount of boat work. We used to go there o – I think it was Thursday evenings and Sunda mornings. Sunday mornings we always used t row up the river, up towards Black Bridge an I can remember once – going up towards th Black Bridge there's lots of sandbanks the and we had to be careful. At the time I was o the tiller, so it was my responsibility to see an obstacles in the way but we got stuck on th sandbanks. Up to our knees in water trying t push this thing off and get it floating agair It was great fun! We also used to do variou fêtes and carnivals and things in the town. had some good times there.

I can remember one particular time we ha to stand on top of the office building ther

hippenham Town AFC in the 1937/38 season.

flat roof building there – where at the begin-
ng of the parade when we get there on the
hursday or the Sunday you have to raise the
nsign. Somebody the other end was raising
e Union flag or Union Jack. At the end of
e evening we had to – we never had buglers
the time when I was there, so they never
ayed *Sunset*. It was just the bosun's pipe,
ey blew the whistle and we withdrew the
nsign down to the bottom there. But I can
member it well, one Sunday morning it was
y turn to raise the ensign. I'd connected it
the line as I thought, but as it was going up
was twisting around so we had to finish it.
Vhen it got to the top I had to whip it down,
ke it off and put it on properly, so it didn't
vist before Mr Cohu saw it, but apparently I
ter found out he already had! He did make
note and he did speak to me later on. But

that was the fun bit. It was a bit hairy up on
top of that thing there!

Derek Brinkworth

Playing in hob-nail boots

I did play football for the house at school and
I also played football for the Sunday school
team. But other than that it was just kicking
round the street, or things like that. We went
to Calne and played a Sunday school there
and so it was a sort of Sunday school league.
I certainly didn't have any proper boots, we
actually played with hob-nail boots, you know
if somebody had proper football boots they
were considered to be really wealthy. You just
played in your hob-nails which you wore to
school.

Alan Horner

The Western League

In the early days we used to watch Chippenham Town Football Club and there was some characters there and there was a chap named Godfrey Rowlings. In those days, when I was under ten, he played on the left wing for Chippenham. Used to go to the football – Western League I think it was called – because occasionally we had teams from London, Slough. Some quite good teams used to come occasionally – not in the league, but friendly or cup matches. In those days there were a lot of RAF and forces people around here and I think Bath City had a terrific side during the war. I mean if the professionals were stationed round here, they used to play for the local clubs.

David Hall

A keen rivalry

There was rivalry between the Chippenham football clubs – Chippenham United and Chippenham Town. Chippenham United only set up in 1948 I believe, or something like that. It only set up because they wanted to turn professional, but the people down at Chippenham Town didn't want to turn professional. They wanted to keep it an amateur side so some of them broke away and set up Chippenham United to become a professional side. It obviously turned out to be quite a reasonably successful side as far as the locals were concerned. So Chippenham Town had no alternative but to turn professional as well. For a few years there was quite a good ding-dong between the two sides. There was quite a lot of interest and the gates in both Chippenham Town and Chippenham United, it was nothing unusual – when they played one another, and certainly when they played Trowbridge and Salisbury – to get three thousand plus in the grounds, which was a lot of people in such a small, confined space. The grounds were not really equipped to hold three thousand. They could

get a thousand in there reasonably comfortab[le] but once you're cramming three thousand there – that was a lot of people! Chippenha[m] United's ground was where Queen's Cresce[nt] is in Chippenham, off of Hungerdown La[ne] and the Town still played on the Town on th[e] grass – a nice pitch Chippenham Town.

The best player that ever played [for] Chippenham was Kenny Davies – he play[ed] for Chippenham Town, and there was Jo[e] Boyd who played centre half. At Chippenha[m] United there was Kevin McLoughlin, w[ho] played in goal. Jack Preece was centre half.

I think the first time United played t[he] Town, they beat them 4-1. It was quite [a] comprehensive victory, so the Town had [to] strengthen their side, which they subsequent[ly] did. The Town were the premier side becau[se] they had the money behind them, but Unite[d] set a standard which the Town had to come [up] to. Then as time went by, the United fell aw[ay] and they had to pack up, but Chippenha[m] Town still goes on. It was always an occasi[on] when they played one another and obvious[ly] when they played Trowbridge Town and team[s] like Salisbury as well.

Norman Stac[e]

The 'Pie Race'

I used to do a lot of timekeeping for ro[ad] walking. The Chippenham to Calne ro[ad] walk started in Calne and it was just a sm[all] race, mostly Trowbridge and Calne peop[le] Trowbridge Athletic Club – they had a wal[k]ing section and they took an interest and [it] was mostly those people that started it in 195[?] – I think. They had two races in that year an[d] then it just grew and grew and at the height [of] its popularity they used to have coach loads [of] competitors come in from London, Leiceste[r] all over the place – even Guernsey. We've ha[d] them from abroad as well. Mostly people use[d] to call it the 'Pie Race', because the winnin[g]

an Swallow competes in the Chippenham to Calne
d race in 1962.

um had the Harris's trophy and Harris's used
give four big gala pies for the team win-
rs. I think the most we've had is about 250
mpetitors in the event, but gradually road
alking lost its popularity and you haven't
t the stars like you used to have, like Don
hompson and all those sort of people.

Don Little

he travelling pantomime

went to the cinema when I was young,
e one up Station Hill. Of course all silent
ctures. The first time I can remember going
ere I was absolutely terrified! I sat down on
e floor with my head under the seat and
ouldn't budge! I would have been about four
five. I just remember horrible things that
ere happening! Mother said after it really
asn't a suitable picture to have taken me to.

I know I was always taken to see the Charlie
Chaplin pictures, films. I can remember going
to the pantomimes. Every Christmas they had
a pantomime there – that was a great thing!
That was a really big event in our lives, to go
to the pantomime. The travelling pantomime
used to come for about a fortnight and go
on somewhere else. Of course nowadays they
would seem awfully amateurish things, but in
those days they were wonderful.

Elizabeth Perrett

Making your own entertainment

You just made your own entertainment, we
were all young families in the street then and
you just made your own fun and games, either
out in the street or up in the park. Over in
the fields at the back, we would go over there
lighting fires and doing different things. There
was nothing organised. I remember going to
Toc H, round the back of St Mary Street, but
I was never in any youth club as such. Course,
to start with, the cinema was up Station Hill.
I remember we used to go there.

John Lovelock

Going to the pictures

I remember when the Palace came, because
when I went to Ivy Lane I think we used to
have treats once a year. We'd go to the cinema
about Christmas time. That was a chap named
Falls, he was the manager and then when they
built the Gaumont, I think he took that man-
agership as well and the other place closed.
When we were at school we used to go occasionally to the one in Station Hill, only went
there a few times. When I was in my teens I
used to go to the Astoria and the Gaumont.
It was cowboy stuff in those days, and science
and mad scientists and inventions as well. All
black and white of course.

David Hall

Day trip to the Isle of Wight, organised by the Gaumont cinema in the late 1950s.

The Saturday morning show

Saturday morning pictures at the Gaumont. That was a ritual that children went through in those days and was a release from our parents. I guess we would walk through the town to the Gaumont for Saturday morning pictures. Harry Falls was the guy who ran the Picture Palace, originally in Station Hill, which was also a skating rink. Anyway that was Saturday mornings. They were mainly cowboy films if I remember rightly. I guess they would have been that sort of film. But it was like a club. You joined and you participated in something on the stage. I think the stage was probably mainly for birthdays. So if your birthday came around you were invited onto the stage, Mr Falls would have gone through some game procedure and I guess everybody was a winner.

Tony Knee

Rock around the clock

You had the two cinemas. You had the Gaumont, then you had the Astoria. And you had films changing – the Gaumont would have two changes of film, I think they used to change on Sundays and Wednesdays, something like that, so you had plenty of films you could go to. I used to go quite regularly and used to enjoy them. You know I saw this Bill Hayley Rock around the Clock thing, I can remember that and being musically minded, I suppose that sort of stuck in my mind. New kind of music, you know, a new life…

Alan Horn

The Victory Parade

The earliest memory that I can pinpoint was the Victory or Peace Parade after the First World War. Father drove a horse and cart down the little slipway – by the old Co-op can remember it there – absolutely pouring with rain and being covered up and just seeing a few brightly-coloured wagons going down the street.

Chippenham Horse Show was always a great event. That's built over now where the football ground is. Yewstock Crescent was fields, open fields all the way down. That's where they used to hold the horse show. That was a great event. Used to drive in round-abouts and coconut shies. My brother always managed one or two coconuts. All that sort of things. Mother always used to buy honey there – honey in the comb. Men taking their honey. You know – all competitions, vegetables, fruit and everything. A very big affair. The jumping and the ordinary events they have nowadays. It was a lovely day – look forward to it weeks ahead, when it was going to be Chippenham Show.

Elizabeth Perrett

Scout camp at Easton Grey

When our Scout master was called up for the Navy, Mr Peter Mortimore, well known as the local coal merchant, took over running the Scout troop and a very good job he made of it too. We managed to go to camp. Easter and Whitsun we used to camp locally at Ford or different places. One time – I think 1942 – we had quite a spectacular camp. One of our members, his family had a farm at Dursley, place called Uley near Dursley. Peter Mortimore was a man of many ideas and things. He worked out a system where we could hike there. It was to be done in two days. The first journey from Chippenham to Easton Grey. We camped on the Easton Grey estate. Second day was from Easton Grey to Dursley. Approximately ten miles a day. Those ten miles were broken up into three sections – we had two carts, the big, one we used to call the old trek cart. That carried our heavy equipment,

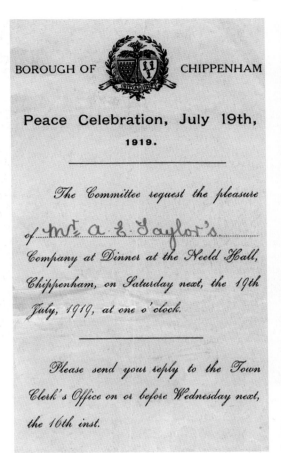

Invitation to the Borough of Chippenham Peace Celebration, 19 July 1919, held at the Neeld Hall.

tents, cooking utensils and things, and we had a smaller handcart, that two or more people got in. One section had cycles – there were about eight in a section, so each ten miles each day – you pulled the trek cart for one section, small handcart for second and you had a rest for cycling on the third section!

Frank White

Fond memories of Scouting

I became a Cub Scout and a lot of my child-hood was spent involved with the Scouting movement. And that was 1st Chippenham and

Crowds gather in the rain for the Peace Day service, in the Market Place, July 1919.

I guess they are still around and this was in the Woodlands Road area I suppose. Fond memories of Scouting and fond memories of a lot of people there, mostly of my age, but also Skip Robinson. He was such a kind gentleman and always very helpful. So I suspect other people will probably remember Skip Robinson. I stayed in scouting until I was fifteen.

Tony Knee

Leading the Guards

In 1960 the lady who had been doing the Guides wanted to give up so I took over as Guide Captain of the Salvation Army Guides. In the Salvation Army, I had been what they called Girl Guards. They had a different set up. They called their little Brownies Sunbeams and they were in yellow and the older girls were in grey. They were Guards, but they based it o the same thing as Girl Guides and Brownies. was quite easy and we had some fun.

We went down one day as a trip to Swanag and we went across to Brownsea Island wher Guiding started. Lovely sanctuary over ther and they enjoyed that. Oh yes we used to g off all over the place. Billycans, tying knot and making rope ladders to have fun wit and we went off one year to the Salvatio Army headquarters for this sort of thing .. they've got a place quite near London and it beautiful grounds and you stay in huts and m husband came with me as well, because th gentleman who was the Army Captain at th time, wanted a bit of help. We made up rop ladders and things to loop across and the enjoyed every minute of it. My husband ha helped them put together this assault cours

t Chippenham Boy Scouts and Cubs, pictured outside the Scout hut in Audley Road, in the early 1930s.

sorts. They had all taken to him really well. hey thought he was lovely, because he was illing, even at a much older age than them id me, to get in touch and get involved and ave some fun with them. When we were icking up on the Sunday when we were ming home, they had water things – I don't iow where they had got them from like ueegee things from washing-up liquid and ey were soaking him! Not content with that ey then came out with a bucket and they ere soaking him and he had to go and get imself completely changed in the end. They ved him to bits and they showed it in that ay. We had some laughs!

Marian Stickland

rummer with the band

ly father, Arthur Little, was always musi- lly minded and if it hadn't been for his rents he would have gone in the Army I think – as a bandsman. He was a member of the old Chippenham British Legion Band, which during the war was mostly formed as the Home Guard Band and he was the big drummer. Also he's been the bass drummer for the Chippenham Silver Band, which is the predecessor of the band we've got now. He also played in the Westinghouse Orchestra for some of the time. He started off actually play- ing in the Merrymakers Dance Band, when he was a young boy. Which was a local dance band, went around the areas and that, but he'd always been interested in music.

Don Little

The Chippenham Town Band

I was in the 1st Chippenham Cubs, but they were starting a Boys' Brigade Unit. One of the attractions to me was that they were going to have a drum and bugle band, so I actu- ally left the Cubs and instead of going to the

Scouts I went straight to the Boys' Brigade. But after a year they didn't show any signs of having a drum and bugle band and the Town Band were asking for young people, so I joined the Town Band instead. I played with the old Chippenham Town Silver Band. The conductor's name was Harry Havenand and he actually taught me how to play the cornet. The band had just recently reformed having been the Home Guard Band during the Second World War, and then they reformed as the Chippenham Town Silver Prize Band and they asked for young people and I was one of the young people went forward and I've been connected with playing ever since.

In the early nineties I was looking after the Air Training Corps Band, instructing there, and I felt that there wasn't a need for a Town Band in Chippenham. However, Doug Cleverly kept on and so, I think it was 1992, and we got together, just a small group of us, and decided to get this band going, the Chippenham Town Band. Started off with about eight people at the first rehearsal and, the intention was to start the band as a brass band. But, on that evening, there was more people who could play flutes and clarinets than brass instruments so we had to adapt ourselves to change to become a wind band! For the first night I took some music with me, some hymn books, and the band had great difficulty in playing a hymn together. Now you know, after eleven, twelve years going on, the band is a very competent band, mustering around thirty-four players and they are now able to tackle most music that is produced. Certainly a lot better now from when they couldn't play a hymn together!

Alan Horner

Monkton Park Girls' Club

I was in the Girls' Club, at Monkton church you know. Mrs King used to run it then, and her husband, on the corner of Foghamshir he had the big ironmonger's shop. Every ye they used to put on Gilbert and Sulliva sort of opera. Well I can remember I was two; I was in *Merry England* and *The Pirates Penzance*. We used to have some fun you kno We performed them at the chapel, underneat the chapel they've got their hall. We had a litt children's orchestra, we used to play in th Co-op Hall. I used to play violin. Mr Callaha ran it, it was through the Co-op Society. W used to play in there and we used to go roun to the village halls, playing music.

Freda Cur

Serving with the Red Cross

I belonged to the Red Cross as a junior an as a senior. From that I always wanted to d nursing. So I used to do a few hours voluntar at St Andrew's Hospital when I was abou fourteen, fifteen, sixteen. In those days it w really coming out of the workhouse era. The still had a lot of people up there, misplace people that was in town. There was an ol man that used to walk about the streets an we never knew what his name was, but w used to tease him. And nowadays I would hus anyone I see teasing anybody really. But h used to always take a walk from the hospit and part of his route was up Wood Lane. H never got fed up with us teasing him. He use to chase bigger boys with his walking stic but he was harmless. He worked up there fo years apparently in the canteen, 'cause he pai for his keep that way. But more and more was coming in as a home at the time for ol people, that couldn't look after themselves an more. I can remember one older lady up ther that I used to visit regularly. The Red Cros gave me a good insight of what I wanted t do, my working life.

Peggy Burges

embers of the Monkton Hill Girl's Club perform *The Gondoliers*. Pictured in Monkton Park in 1949.

he Chippenham Hospital Carnival

ourse in those days the big event of the year
as the Flower Show, which was always held
it in the fields at the back there, with big
arquees. The entrance into that was down
e road in Yewstock. That was the entrance
to the fields out there, you know. I can
member Empire Day coming round about
is time of the year, I think it was. It was just
rought home to everyone about the Empire
at we had and all the things about it and
e different flags of the different countries.
ourse every year there was the Carnival – it
as called the Hospital Carnival in those days
d it was run purely for the hospital. That
as always run up in John Coles Park and I
member all the nurses used to be up there
ith stalls and things like that and all the pro-
eeds went to the hospital. I think everyone
rned out for it in those days. It was well
pported, there was the processions – horse
d carts in those days.

John Lovelock

Members of the Chippenham Juniors of the Red Cross
in the late 1940s, pictured with Mrs Thatcher, the
Commandant.

Display by Milsom's hairdressers at the Neeld Hall to celebrate the engagement of Princess Elizabeth and Prince Phil in 1946.

Visiting the villages

We used to have a carnival before the war, for years. And it was a great thing. The week before the actual carnival, they used to come out round the villages with their collection boxes and they'd come up to Kington, up the street with the music and all these people in their fancy dress, sloshing their buckets at you. But unfortunately they never stayed long enough for you to really appreciate them! They just rushed up through, but it was always a great event. The village people were all out watching. Yes it was very good before the war. I think we used to have much better ones. The Nestlé's factory always used to be very good. After the war, that's when it started to fade away.

Elizabeth Perrett

Charging the accumulators

I suppose I was round about six or seven, can remember father bringing a wireless hom then. They were all battery operated wi accumulators and there was a shop – Sne it was called. It was down by the old Tow Council offices, well there were shops ther Pierce's, an upholstery shop. But there was th garage-cum-shop down there where you too your accumulators and had them charged u

John Lovelo

Our first TV

Before the war, we had a very small TV inco porated in a large radio. The pictures wou just come and go. My father put a pole u to get the signal from London. Of course th

V part of it was shut down at the beginning
' the war, but we continued to listen to the
dio and my father would tune in the short
ave. I can remember Lord Haw-Haw. Father
so built a radiogram and I would curl up
' the speaker and listen to *Children's Hour,
ncle Mac*. In the 1950s we were the first one
have a TV in Chippenham. Not as small
the one we had before the war and not
te today's. We again had a very tall aerial on
e roof. One night it bent over and my par-
its were out and a neighbour tied it down.
uring the coronation our house was full of
ighbours.

Shirley Ritchens

earning to dance

/e went to clubs run by a Reverend Frank
ay that was in St Paul's hall. That was nice.
used to like dancing and we used to get
vitations from the RAF camps at Compton
asset. The list would go up at the Telephone
xchange of dancing – certain dates, anyone
ishing to go put their names down and they
ways use to provide the buses to take us there
id bring us back.

just picked the dancing up myself, the
iodern, but the old time we went to classes
: Kington Langley and that's where I met
iy husband! He lived at Kington Langley,
iat's where we met. Actually last year, last
)ctober, we had an invitation to go back
i Kington Langley for an old-time dance,
ecause the class that we actually were in
ras celebrating their sixtieth anniversary and
i they had this dance. They had a cake and
ifreshments and wine and it was a lovely,
ively evening and they invited so many
lder people that used to go, but don't go
iow and it was lovely to meet up with them
ir the first time in years. We really enjoyed
, a lovely, lovely time.

Jean Brind

Tony Wootton dressed for the carnival, *c.* 1938.

Apple Blossom Time

I did go to dancing lessons when I was sixteen. That was down the other end of the
town –Woodlands Hall or somewhere down
that side. I always remember the first dance
I learnt was the waltz and that was to *Apple
Blossom Time*. 'I'll be with you in apple blossom time…' That was the first dance I learnt,
because apparently the waltz is quite easy to
learn. And then you went to dances and you
sort of picked it up as you went along. If you
happened to have a good dancer, you know, a
fella, because the fellas lead, and you followed
them … then you did pick it up as you went
along. That was all the dancing lessons I had
when I was young.

Peggy Chamberlain

A group gathers outside the Lowden School for the first Chippenham Carnival after the Second World War.

Members of the Telephone Exchange taking part in the carnival, sponsored by Knights Castille Soap, in the early 1950s.

Old-time dancing at the Neeld Hall, organised by Westinghouse in the 1950s.

ronation day

 mother and I would go for walks, along
terdown, Hungerford Lane – all were
ds. Ladyfield had just been built and at the
 they built prefabs to house the people
n Bristol. In 1936 it was all fields. During
 celebrations for the Coronation of King
orge VI, all the children paraded around
field in fancy dress. My mother had made
 a red, white and blue dress. The bodice
 made out of a flag with the king and
en's heads on it. Another walk we did was
to Rowden Lane to the farm. Through
ds of wild flowers and grasses. In the
 to the entrance to Rowden Farm was a
non ball from Civil War times. One time
emember we heard that the farmer was
shing corn, and a group of children from
vden went up to watch, me included. And
 were covered in dust! I had a new gab-

ardine mac on and when I got home my
mother was very cross!

Shirley Ritchens

Collecting stars

Behind Ivy Lane School it was all fields, right
until you got to Downing Street, because the
council houses then hadn't been built and
right behind Cowleaze Terrace there were
no houses. I think there was a garden centre
sort of thing, sold vegetables and things. Then
beyond that, were fields for cows. All along
Hungerdown Lane it was lovely cornfields.
Beautiful waving corn. Beautiful fields. Of
course in the holiday times, I remember an
aunt used to come and stay with us. She'd collect all the children, most of them in the street
I should think, brothers and sisters, and she'd
take us for a long walk. That was for the moth-

Audrey, Robert, Mary and Marguerite Thomas dressed up for the Langley Burrell School celebration of George V's Jubilee in 1936.

ers to get rid of their children for a while, so they could get on with their work! I remember very well, she used to take us to Holy Well and right out nearly to Biddestone. We crossed the field until we came to some boulders and a little brook. Only a small brook, streamlet thing, with the boulders round it. We used to sit on these stones and have our lunch. Be tired of the journey, but it really was lovely. We'd gather what we called the stars – they were very, very tiny. Not as big as a fingernail. Very small, I don't quite know how they got there, but that's the only place that you could find these stars. I don't know how the stars collected or how they formed. It really was exciting. And we had games, and before we went home we would collect stars and bring them home, and that was wonderful. But we walked all that way. There were no bicycles, no cars, nothing in those days.

Amy Brand

An interest in photography

I used to be a member of the Chippenh. Camera Club, who used to meet in old Community Centre at the end Lowden Avenue, which is now pulled dov We had our own darkroom there and used to have meetings – I think once month. We used to have the darkroom the which we could hire out and use whene we wanted to and I used to spend hours there developing and messing about w photographs and that. Then I took up cir photography.

Don L

The Stamp Club

The only club I ever joined was the Star Club. Children's Stamp Club. Used to m here in these buildings here. A gentleman Mr Williams, ran it. We met on a mont

committee of the Chippenham Flower Show in around 1908, with the Reverend Henslowe seated second from right.

sis. I was in the Junior Stamp Club and ʈen in the proper Chippenham Philatelic ⸬ciety.

Norman Stacey

fascinating collection

hen I was a youngster Nan gave me a ˌmp collection. I was quite interested, but ⸬ a grown-up you take a different view, a ⸬ious view of stamp collecting and I got ˌite hooked on it. I joined the local society ⸬hich in those days – you were talking about ˌenty, twenty-five members. We used to meet ⸬ one of the small rooms in the Town Hall ⸬d later on at the library. My main interest ⸬as a small south Atlantic Island – Tristan da ˌunha. My brother-in-law, who's a botanist, ⸬ went on an expedition there 1957 – and ⸬'s been there several times since. I had quite ⸬ good collection of old letters. Mind there

were not that many people there that can write to start with and there were not many ships that call to pick up letters. I did have quite a good collection, but I sold that and I branched out into the Channel Islands. When I first looked at the Channel Islands, I thought there won't be very much, just the issue – the occupation issues – and that there wouldn't be very much to collect. But by gosh how wrong I was! I've been at it for years. One thing about the Channel Islands, when they were occupied during the war, there was no direct communication from or to the islands. The only means of communication was by Red Cross messages, where they could only send one message a month and each message was only twenty-five words. So if you wrote to your friend or relative in the islands, they sent a reply on the reverse of it.

Frank White

Postcard view of the open-air pool at Monkton Park.

The joys of a car

When we first married, I used to borrow my father's car. It was an old Morris 1000. No heaters, no radios or anything like that and to start it on a cold morning you had a manual choke. It would either go or it wouldn't! You had a starting handle to crank it over to get it to start. I can remember going to Swindon with my wife on a freezing cold winter's day and by the time we got there my feet were numb. My wife was lucky because she had a blanket over her legs and we were glad to get out the car and go somewhere and get a cup of tea or something to warm up.

In the Morris 1000 you had four speeds. If you were going along at fifty miles an hour, the engine was screaming away. It's a dreadful noise. If you came to a hill, you had to change all the way down and sometimes you may have to go down to first. Of course, from second gear to the first gear there was no

synchromesh, so you had to double declut Luckily, I learnt with British Telecom. I to go on a week's driving tuition and learnt on a smallish lorry. No synchrom whatsoever. A four speed diesel, very n very heavy. So the things we were taught how to change down in the gears, to dou declutch and I got into the habit of it ev with the modern synchromesh ones. Whe eventually got a car of my own, which wa Ford Anglia, I used to double declutch in th but there was no need to, it was a habit you into! But that was a better car because it ha heater and it also had a radio! Then my seco car was a Ford Cortina, estate, but again it a lot better. A lot stronger, powerful and v nice car and I had that when I had my t children. We used to go out everywhere. used to go out camping with the estate car, it all in there and away you go. Great fun.

Derek Brinkwo